UN-NATURAL DISASTER

Stories of Survival after the Graniteville Train Tragedy

UN-NATURAL DISASTER

N.J. Nidiffer

AUGUSTA

UN-NATURAL DISASTER
By Nina Nidiffer
A Harbor House Book/2005

For information address:
HARBOR HOUSE
111 TENTH STREET
AUGUSTA, GEORGIA 30901

Jacket photo by Nina Nidiffer..

Library of Congress Cataloging-in-Publication Data

Nidiffer, N. J. (Nina J.)
Un-natural disaster : stories of survival after the
Graniteville train tragedy / N.J. Nidiffer.
p. cm.
Includes bibliographical references and index.
ISBN 1-891799-29-0 (paper back : alk. paper)
1. Railroad accidents--South Carolina--Graniteville.
I. Title.
HE1781.G73N53 2005
363.12'2'0975775--dc22

2005011721

Printed in the United States of America

10 9 8 7 6 5 4 3 2 1

This book is dedicated to
the people of Graniteville and
to the first responders who came
to our aid when we needed them most.

ACKNOWLEDGEMENTS

On the afternoon of January 6, 2005, I watched with pride, but no great surprise, as Graniteville and its surrounding communities rallied to cope with a railroad accident and chemical spill that claimed nine lives.

I determined to write about that disaster, but not in a step-by-step analysis of what went wrong and why. Rather, I wished to assemble a handful of personal stories of men and women — Avondale employees, Graniteville residents and first responders — who were affected by the crash and the terrible spill that followed.

A wealth of gratitude to:

Aiken County Sheriff's Office
Aiken Emergency Management Division
Aiken Public Works
Barnwell County Sheriff's Office
Barnwell Emergency Management Agency
Edgefield County Sheriff's Office
Allendale County Sheriff's Office
Allendale Emergency Management Agency
Lexington County Sheriff's Office
Richmond County Sheriff's Office
Richmond Emergency Services Division
McCormick County Sheriff's Office
Orangeburg County Sheriff's Office
Columbia and Augusta/Richmond Counties in Georgia
Richmond County Animal Control
Orangeburg County Animal Control
Greenwood County Sheriff's Office

Special thanks to:

Graniteville-Vaucluse-Warrenville Fire Department
Belvedere Fire Department
Merriwether Fire Department

Sage Mill Fire Department
Aiken Public Safety Department
North Augusta Public Safety Department
Bath Fire Department
Langley Fire Department
Augusta-Richmond County (Ga.) Fire Department
Aiken HAZMAT Team
Aiken COBRA Team
Lexington County Fire Service
Aiken County Emergency Management Services
Belvedere Rescue Squad
Aiken Rescue Squad
Jackson Rescue Squad
Palmetto Ambulance Service
Regional Ambulance Service
Gold Cross Ambulance Service
Capital City Ambulance Service
Williston Rescue Squad
Edgefield Emergency Management Services

In addition, sincere appreciation goes to:

South Carolina Governor's Office
South Carolina Emergency Management Division
Chief Information Office
Office of Regulatory Staff
Department of Health and Environmental Control
State Law Enforcement Department
Labor Licensing Regulation
South Carolina Highway Patrol
South Carolina Sate Transport Police
Department of Natural Resources
South Carolina Department of Transportation
South Carolina Department of Education
South Carolina Fire Academy
South Carolina State Guard
Department of Mental Health

Police departments of:

New Ellenton, Cayce, West Columbia, Columbia,
Burnettown, North Augusta, Aiken,
University of South Carolina Aiken, Edgefield,
McCormick, Charleston, Johnston, Orangeburg,
Wackenhut Savannah River Site and Lexington

Aiken City Animal Control
North Augusta Animal Control

Also, thanks to:

National Transportation and Safety Bureau,
Environmental Protection Agency,
Federal Emergency Management Agency Region IV,
Federal Bureau of Investigation,
Fort Gordon, Federal Railroad Administration,
U.S. Coast Guard, U.S. Postal Service Inspector,
Center for Disease Control,
Occupational Safety and Health Administration,
the American Red Cross, the Salvation Army,
Norfolk Southern Railroad, Olin, BellSouth, Motorola,
the coroner's offices of Aiken, Richmond, Barnwell and
Edgefield counties.

To you — and to all those who deserve recognition, but who were overlooked in the controlled chaos of the first response — a heartfelt thank you.

I would also like to personally thank the people who entrusted me with their stories, as well as those who continue to encourage each other through the on-going aftermath of the disaster.

We stumble. But we do not fall.

N.J. Nidiffer

CONTENTS

AIKEN CHAIRMAN SPEAKS OUT

BETWEEN 2:45 AND 3 A.M. JANUARY 6, 2005, most of the citizens of Graniteville, South Carolina, slept, thus unaware and unprepared for the danger lurking in the darkness.

I certainly commend Nina Nidiffer for her effort to tell the story of the people of Graniteville and the impact this event had, and continues to have, on their lives.

The accident, a head-on train collision involving many cars, included three cars carrying 90 tons each of deadly chlorine gas. The impact caused some of the train cars to be stacked, including the three that held the toxic gas.

One ruptured, releasing more than 70 tons of noxious fumes into the environment.

This disaster hit home and I can certainly identify with those directly affected. My brother, Ronnie, lost his 24-year-old grandson, John Laird, Jr. His family and friends will always remember him.

Another brother, Cecil, has a son, Mike, who worked at "ground zero" — the Steam Plant of Avondale Mills. Mike survived, but still has breathing problems.

All told, nine individuals lost their lives and some 300 were injured. Their lives and the lives of all Graniteville residents will forever be impacted by this early morning tragedy.

Later in the day, a House colleague, Representative Skipper Perry, and I went up in a S.C. Law Enforcement Division helicopter. As we flew over Graniteville and the crash site, I reflected on what a normal day would have been.

The streets would have been busy with cars, trucks and school buses. Local businesses and factories would have been up and running. The shopping center would have been crowded with shoppers.

Leavelle McCampbell Middle and Byrd Elementary would be filled with hundreds of students and staff, near what was now ground zero.

As I looked down from the helicopter, there was no movement except for the occasional HAZMAT person monitoring the release of deadly gas and searching for victims' bodies. I saw nothing else moving. It was a scary feeling. I cannot explain all I felt as I looked down on the still, silent community. It was eerie.

Mike Craig, a worker at the steam plant, escaped after climbing to the roof of the plant. He went on to crawl under a fence, struggling onward until someone picked him up, transported him for decontamination, and later to the Aiken hospital for treatment.

The events of January 6, 2005, will always be on my mind, and as I drive through the community of Graniteville. The eerie feeling always returns.

Good came out of this tragedy. Fire departments, law enforcement agencies and HAZMAT from all over South Carolina and from Richmond County, Georgia, worked together in a spirit of cooperation and caring.

The Department of Social Services and Department of Health and Environmental Control, South Carolina and Aiken County Emergency Preparedness Agencies, Avondale Mills and its chairman and CEO were present to offer their aid and assistance.

The American Red Cross and local businesses provided meals to the workers, who worked tirelessly day and night.

Aiken County Sheriff Michael Hunt and his department, together with the Graniteville Volunteer Fire Department, under the leadership of Chief Phil Napier, worked countless hours to rescue and recover those unable to escape. They did not rest until all bodies were recovered.

The decision to evacuate the affected citizens in order to ensure their safety was a difficult one. However,

police and fire departments from across the state converged on Graniteville to help local officials safely effect the evacuation.

Some residents were able to stay with relatives or in nearby hotels and motels. Others found themselves in shelters around the county.

The Aiken County Delegation worked to provide support and assistance to those folks who bore the responsibility of protecting our citizens. They did a fantastic job. Their role was one of support and they excelled, contacting Washington, D.C., for assistance, communicating with the National Highway and Transportation Safety Board and Norfolk Southern Railroad, and mainly talking to the citizens to direct them where and how to obtain the assistance they needed.

We really do not know the long-term impact this disaster will have. We do know that had it not been for the grace of God, many more lives might have been lost.

I recommend this book not only as a literary work, but also for its historical importance to our community. God bless you as you read these pages.

To Nina Nidiffer, thank you for your hard work putting this book together.

Representative J. Roland Smith
Chairman of the Aiken County Legislative Delegation
Lifelong resident of the Graniteville, South Carolina
March 31, 2005

A SOUTH CAROLINA SENATOR'S VIEW

MORE THAN 150 YEARS AGO, the village of Graniteville, South Carolina was founded. While begging forgiveness to any possible omission of facets in history, one might say the railways led to the development and growth of this small community, and their impact on Graniteville's modern history has been profound.

In general, railways have played and continue to play a vital role in small-town South Carolina, transforming us from an agrarian state to a manufacturing- and tourism-based economy. Within that thought, two important things are noted: community and economy, both of which were threatened by the great tragedy that occurred January 6, 2005.

I have lived my entire life in the Horse Creek Valley area of Aiken County and possess very fond memories — boyhood through adulthood — to show for it. I will tell you, the events that occurred earlier this year caused me to reflect on what we truly have here in Aiken County.

As a young boy I remember the community through the eyes of an early-morning paper delivery. I remember days in Little League Baseball and as an athlete at Langley-Bath-Clearwater High School. I remember my mother working third shift at Hickman Mills.

As a young man and father, I remember the security I felt raising a family in this area. On into my political career, I remember many individuals whose encouragement and support led me to Columbia to represent this area of our state in the South Carolina Legislature.

To think that a tragedy such as this might create a

situation whereby others might not be afforded the opportunities to have such wonderful experiences and develop similar memories is distressing.

However, once again, we neighbors pulled together and came through it. The same support I felt as a young boy active in sports, as a young adult and family man, and as a yearling in politics lives strong and has carried this area of our state through one of its most difficult moments in history.

Even though our sense of community held us strong, one cannot deny the reality of how a tragedy such as this affects the backbone of the economy. In addition to the disruptions in personal lives, which there were many, the business community was direly affected and has held strong.

From the sudden closure of many businesses for more than a week to the daily aftermath, the economy in this portion of Aiken County was hit very hard.

As a small businessman, I can attest to the fact that any unforeseen closure and unmitigated interruption in production is a direct hit on the business, and therefore, the employees. Combine that with an ill nationwide economy struggling to recover, and you may have another tragedy.

However, I believe that in this, too, we have seen how "adversity breeds strength," and I trust that good things will happen to great people and this great place.

While the appearance of Graniteville may have changed throughout the years and through this tragedy, the character will always remain the same. Everyone who reads this book and comes to understand the circumstances surrounding those early morning events in January 2005 will benefit in a very significant way.

In the time of crisis, a divergent group of individuals,

spanning many entities of government and community, united for a common cause. My lasting memories will not be about individuals, but about teamwork.

There is no way to name all who should be recognized for their time, their insights, and their unforgettable bravery. Those with the superb leadership skills, those with the utterly fearless commitment, those with the focus to serve and protect others, and those with the countless gestures of encouragement have been essential in this effort and have secured a place in history and in the hearts of the community.

Now through the pages of this book you, too, will learn about the strong-willed and extraordinarily dedicated individuals, those who faced tragedy and did not walk away in fear.

Senator Thomas L. Moore
District 25
Aiken, Edgefield, Saluda
and McCormick counties
March 31, 2005

AUGUSTA MAYOR, ON THE RECORD

CYCLOHEXANE. ANHYDROUS AMMONIA. Potassium Hydroxide. Ferric Chloride. These are just some of the hazardous chemicals that move through our cities in railroad cars on a regular basis.

Dozens more strange names complete the list. CSX Transportation alone accounted for nearly 5,000 separate shipments through Augusta, Georgia in 2003.

Chemicals drive our manufacturing economy. Trains and trucks move them. We trust the private sector to move and store these volatile mixtures safely. We trust the government to insure the rules are followed. Most of the time, everything works the way it is supposed to.

Sometimes, though, something goes wrong.

A lot went terribly wrong the night of January 6, 2005 in the small town of Graniteville, South Carolina. When a freight training towing three tank cars of chlorine hit another train parked on a siding, one car was ripped open, allowing a cloud of death to migrate through the town, invading homes, businesses and factories. For many people there was no escape.

What happened to our neighbors a few miles across the Savannah River had the effect of the detonation of a weapon of mass destruction. Many people died, hundreds sought medical treatment and thousands were chased out of their homes.

U.S. Senator Lindsey Graham said the residents' "lives were turned upside down."

The call for help brought first responders and equipment from cities scores of miles away. Under the leadership of

Augusta Emergency Management Agency Director Howard Willis, the City of Augusta provided co-ordination for the HAZMAT responders.

Chief Willis, a veteran city fireman better known as "Bubber," is no stranger to cataclysmic events. In the days after the World Trade Center attack in 2001, he and I were at ground zero with cash donations from the greater Augusta area that totaled $1.2 million. The New Yorkers appreciated the support. Bubber and I came away with a new appreciation for an event of mass destruction.

Three years later, we were together in Central Florida to deliver financial assistance and tractor-trailer loads of water to residents who had been assaulted by three successive hurricanes. The chief and I came to understand all over again how a single event can devastate a community.

So, when the call came from Graniteville, Chief Willis knew what lay ahead. More than 50 first responders from Augusta participated in support activities, joining a list of local, state and federal agencies that covers three typed pages.

Mayors like to spend their time courting new business investment in their cities. We also like to know the water is flowing, the trash is being picked up and the potholes are filled it. But, since September 11, 2001, we spend more and more time and effort worrying about the safety of our citizens. And, freight trains are on the agenda.

One month after the September 11th attacks, more than 200 mayors, fire and police chiefs and emergency managers gathered in Washington, D.C. to put together our agenda for Homeland Security. We knew our police, fire and emergency medical technicians – our first responders – were the troops on the front line for Homeland Security. We know our citizens and institutions are the new targets of opportunity.

From that meeting came the National Action Plan for Safety and Security in America's Cities. One of the major issues identified was "freight rail security."

Our recommendation was: "Freight railroads should be required to develop new notification procedures and to provide better information to the local jurisdictions through which they will be transporting chemicals and other hazardous materials."

The second recommendation was: "Improved notification and information should extend to the storage of freight on sidings and to other practices that could pose risks to immediate neighborhoods and major local assets and venues."

Meeting in Washington, D.C., within days of the Graniteville accident, more than 50 mayors renewed their call for this protection for their cities in letters to Secretary of Transportation Norman Mineta and Secretary of Homeland Security Tom Ridge.

The following month, Senator Charles Schumer of New York and Senator Graham, introduced a bill to improve railroad safety by increasing fines for accidents and requiring advance notification of shipments.

According to the Association of American Railroads, about 20 percent of all chemical tonnage and virtually all chlorine are shipped by rail. That represents 1.7 million carloads of hazardous materials annually.

The railroads have a lot at stake, and they don't like people meddling in their business. They have rejected outright the mayors' requests. Norfolk Southern's Vice President, Joel Harrell, III cites "Federal preemption" and "security reasons."

Those arguments are weak at best, considering it took first responders to the Graniteville crash about a half hour to confirm they had a leak of chlorine.

The railroads say crews have a list of all cars on the trail, and the content of each car is clearly marked on a placard. But what if the crew is disabled, or the wreck is not immediately assessable?

CSX Transportation has argued the security angle in opposing advance notification and uses an example where such information was improperly made public. However, in the example cited, the information came from a disgruntled CSX Transportation employee. One the other hand, cities handle sensitive Homeland Security information everyday without compromise.

The railroads say they don't want to have to fax a manifest of their trains to every city along the track. They know that is an absurd statement. With the technology available today, this information can be quickly and effortlessly sent anywhere. We are currently using such a notification system for the shipment of nuclear waste.

The City Council in Washington, D.C., has taken the argument one step further by adopting an ordinance that bans these rail shipments of hazardous waste through the city. That is the same position taken by the Centers for Disease Control, which recommends routing hazardous materials "away from densely populated areas, where feasible."

Rerouting, though, doesn't solve the problem; it simply moves it to some other official's jurisdiction.

In some ways the railroads try to be helpful. CSX Transportation publishes a Hazardous Materials Density Study "for the sole purpose of developing emergency response and contingency plans" in the communities it serves. Unfortunately, those studies have never been provided to our Emergency Management Agency.

Norfolk Southern promotes cities to install Operation Respond Emergency Information System software. Information about the contents of railcars is immediately available, however, the number on the rail car must first be obtained from the crash site in order to be entered into the system.

We know that as long as hazardous chemicals areneeded to drive our economy and sustain our quality of life, railroads will be called up to ship them. Public officials must do everything we can to see these materials are shipped in the safest possible environment and that our first responders have the best information, training and equipment available.

Some help is on the way. In 2003, the Department of Transportation issued HM 232, which requires shippers and carriers of hazardous materials to develop security plans to assess their risks and plan responses. The railroads should voluntarily share this information with first responders.

In 2004, the Department of Transportation and Department of Homeland Security jointly requested comments for ways to improve the rail shipment and security of hazardous material.

And in 2005, HM 223 went into effect to grant local officials more authority and responsibility to regulate railcar storage.

In the days after the Graniteville accident, I attended a funeral for one of the victims, Steven Bagby Sr. He worked the night shift at Avondale Mills and died helping his co-workers escape the chlorine cloud that was enveloping the plant.

At that funeral I saw his son — his first child, Steven Bagby Jr. —— who had been born a handful of days before his father's heroic death.

Those moments in the funeral home chapel showed me those of us in positions of authority carry a great responsibility to go the extra mile, walk the extra step, in the interest of protecting our citizens.

Mayor Bob Young
Augusta, Georgia
March 31, 2005

PROLOGUE

Pray that your flight be not in winter...
for then there will be great tribulation,
such as has not been from the
beginning of the world until now,
no, and never will be.

MATTHEW 24:20-21

THE ROOTS OF THE GRANITEVILLE MILLS sink deep into the blue stone beneath the region's sandy soil. More than a century ago, William Gregg, a visionary who believed the South would be well served to learn the benefits of technology from its northern neighbors, established a village that he meant to serve as a model for what a textile town could be.

He constructed small but sturdy homes, boarding houses, churches and a hotel. He planted a community garden in peaches and pecans. A community school — the Graniteville Academy — ensured the next generation of children would learn to read and write.

Attendance was compulsory for youngsters under twelve. Those who missed classes found their parents were fined a nickel a day — a sum that could make or break a family budget in those days. Truants were rare.

At the village's heart was a mill built of the granite quarried nearby, its foundation stone laid in October 1846. The original mill was a showplace, reminiscent of a modern corporate headquarters, surrounded by lawns, pebbled paths and fountains.

Cotton dust forbade the use of candles or gas lanterns within. Workers instead relied on floor to ceiling windows for light. They worked from "can't see to can't see" — dawn to dusk. But they were paid more money than they could hope to earn tilling farms where the exhausted soil was already beginning to play out.

Much as he admired the technology of the North, William Gregg was a southerner at his core. He was among the signers of the South Carolina Articles of Secession, which justified the state's split with the Federal Union.

As the War Between the States became a reality, Gregg's

mill provided cloth and shirting for Confederate uniforms. He was pardoned for his service with the Confederacy by President Andrew Johnson in 1865, and went on to oversee the continued growth of his mill — and his dream.

A much longed for rail line — the Columbia to Hamburg Railroad (which in turn became Southern Railway) — was finally established in 1867. The Graniteville mills gained their first link with a railroad that would play prominently in their later history.

William Gregg died that same year.

The Graniteville Mill is now Avondale Mills, one of the largest producers of denim in the United States. The mills themselves are greatly changed, with Gregg's showpiece of lawns and fountains replaced with more modern buildings clustered tightly together in a teacup of land on the edge of Horse Creek Valley.

But while the structures they labor within have changed, the people of Graniteville remain much the same. William Gregg would have recognized them. Hardworking. Fiercely loyal to family and community. Independent in mind and spirit. Never broken by circumstance.

On a mild winter morning in 2005, the qualities that make the people of Graniteville what they are were tested as never before.

God willing, they would come out the stronger for it.

DAY 1

JANUARY 6, 2005

WINTER MORNINGS in the South Carolina sand hills are rarely harsh, but the early morning of Thursday, January 6, 2005, was sweeter than usual.

A week-long warming trend had fooled plum trees along U.S. Highway 1 into early bloom. Crocuses peeped up through the loam in the woods that lined Horse Creek. Thrifty souls in the small textile village of Graniteville took advantage of the mild temperatures to turn their thermostats up or turn their heat off altogether. A hardy few slept with their windows open, enjoying a brief harbinger of spring.

Down in the Gregg Plant of Avondale Mills, Lamar Ledford sat with his brown suede jacket draped over the back of his chair, watching the monitors that controlled the plant's Bespoke room.

Gregg was a plant that dyed and finished cloth, a tricky process involving 70 shades of dye. The automated Bespoke system was installed to eliminate the possibility of human error.

Lamar, a big bear of a man with black hair and a beard, was happy to have the work. When the Bespoke system went on line in July 2003, only the 21 workers with the highest seniority kept their jobs. Lamar was twenty-first in line, and figured he'd get busted down from head dye mixer to dye chemical handler — the job he'd started with six years ago when he was 19 years old.

He was right about that. He was demoted. But he made a fair bid for the job of Bespoke operator and got it. He was happy enough with the work, even if it was third shift.

He was a night owl by habit, and working late did have its advantages. There were fewer supervisors, and compared to the scalding heat of South Carolina summers, the relative cool of the midnight to 8 a.m. shift made labor more tolerable.

All in all, Lamar Ledford was satisfied.

He couldn't know that earlier that night, a train crew from Norfolk Southern had committed a human error that automation like the Bespoke system was meant to prevent — but with far deadlier consequences than a batch of ruined cloth.

The three-man crew had failed to turn the manual switch that would guide oncoming trains away from the cars they had parked, and no one had noticed the error.

At 2:30 a.m., a train engineer close to Lamar's own age was hurtling north toward a head-on collision that would slam more than 60 tons of liquid chlorine into the still night air.

And no one could prevent it.

DARK TERRITORY

NORFOLK SOUTHERN ENGINEER Christopher Seeling and his conductor rode easily on Train 192, headed from the Augusta railyard toward downtown Columbia. The 42-car, three-engine train carried a mixed freight, a selection of commodities for customers at the end of the line — paper, kaolin, steel coils — a little bit of this and a little bit of that.

The train was carrying potentially hazardous cargo, too. Sodium hydroxide, a granular corrosive used to make lye; cresol, an oily material often used in disinfectants to treat wood and clean paint brushes; and chlorine, a widely-used industrial chemical carried in liquid form inside pressurized 90-ton tankers.

Of the three, chlorine was the most dangerous by far.

Engineer Seeling and his conductor had no reason to

worry. The night was mild, the weather fair except for a rising fog. They had but a few hours to go before they reached Columbia and home.

But Train 192 was traveling through Dark Territory. The term refers not to weather conditions or the pitch-black night enfolding rural fields and woodlands, but to unsignaled rail lines, such as the one between Augusta, Georgia, and Columbia, South Carolina.

Signaled lines allow a dispatcher in a central location to see and control the status of switches. But, in this case, the Norfolk Southern dispatcher in Greenville could not see or manipulate switches anywhere along the route. Because all of the switches were manual, the Greenville dispatcher had to rely on radio transmissions from train crews to inform him of the status of a particular switch.

Nor did Engineer Seeling have access to sensors that would tell him if the switches ahead of him were set for the primary line or for sidings. Dispatcher and crew alike were essentially running blind.

Christopher Seeling — a 28-year-old resident of West Columbia who loved his job so much he routinely requested extra duty — would have had but seconds to realize that the signal at the Hickman Street crossing was presenting him with a hot red face rather than the white circle he was expecting.

The manual switch had not been tripped. His train was about to leave the primary line to cut onto a siding, where it would collide head-on with a two-car, one-engine train that had been parked there the night before.

He must have seen it coming. He may even have opened his mouth to yell. But there was no time — no time at all — in which to stop.

IMPACT

THE CARS COLLIDED nose to nose at 41 miles per hour. Fourteen railcars tumbled from the tracks, sending metal parts and cargo flying. Some of the cars skidded to a smoking halt around a small Avondale Mills office building located at the Hickman Street crossing, terrifying the sole employee working inside.

Tanker cars are built, as their name implies, like tanks. The three-fourths of an inch steel shell of the inner tank is insulated with four inches of impact resistant corkboard or polyurethane foam, or two inches of four pounds-per-cubic-foot minimum density ceramic fiber.

This insulation is covered by a minimum of two inches of glass fiber, covered yet again by an outer jacket of one-eighth inch steel. The tanker's ends, called heads, are shielded with an additional half-inch of steel. Cars built after 1988 further require a protective coating inside and out.

In short, tankers are designed to survive an accident. But not an accident as severe as this.

The tanker heads are reinforced, because that is where an impact is most likely to occur. In this case, the collision was so violent the railcars turned and tumbled sideways, ripping a 29 inch slit down the side of a 90-ton tanker loaded with liquid chlorine.

Sixty tons of the chemical splashed into the night air and instantly vaporized. Moisture from the early morning fog and the haze rising over Horse Creek and the Graniteville Canal gave the plume a billowing green texture.

The cloud, moving faster than the prevailing wind, rolled out in all directions. The heaviest flow boiled north toward the Stevens Steam Plant. The Woodhead Division was also in its path, and farther up the slope of Marshall Street, the Gregg Plant, as well. Heavy ventilation fans in the plants sucked the vapors indoors.

Tendrils of mist wrapped around the corners of Dale's convenience store, snagged around the newly erected sign of the Taqueria Azteca, and floated over the parking lots of Bush's Seafood and Chevy's Cafe.

Spradley's Texaco was saturated in foggy droplets, as were Saint Paul's Episcopal Church, the Graniteville Post Office, the magistrate court, and dozens of other churches, businesses and residences surrounding the plants.

Drivers who were unlucky enough to be on the road suddenly found themselves engulfed in a choking green haze.

Downtown Graniteville had just been gassed.

FIRST 911 CALL

911 Dispatcher:	Nine-one-one. What is your emergency?
Avondale employee:	Hey, um, I work at data processing in Graniteville.
Dispatcher:	Okay.
Employee:	I think there's been a train wreck.
Dispatcher:	Where at?
Employee:	At Graniteville.
Dispatcher:	Where at in Graniteville?
Employee:	Right there at the Hickman Mill.
Dispatcher:	Hickman Mill?
Employee:	Yeah, please, I'm here by myself...
Dispatcher:	Ma'am?

Employee:	(increasingly frantic) I'm here by myself...
Dispatcher:	Hey, ma'am, hang on a minute, you gotta tell where it's at.
Employee:	I went to the end of the building and I see smoke. I can't see anything.
Dispatcher:	Okay. Is it right there where the rail road crossing is?
Employee:	Yeah, right there at Graniteville.
Dispatcher:	Which railroad crossing?
Employee:	Hickman Street.
Dispatcher:	Hickman Street crossing?
Employee:	Oh God, I smell smoke!
Dispatcher:	Okay ma'am...
Employee:	I gotta get out of here!
Dispatcher:	Is there smoke in the building?

The line went dead.

RELEASE

THE THUNDER OF THE CRASH brought wakeful residents out onto their porches and lawns. George Spruell, a former chemistry teacher, saw a green cloud boiling up the gorge toward Powell Street and shouted at his neighbors to get inside.

"Get in the house!" he yelled. "Turn off your ventilation!"

He knew chlorine when he saw it, and he was quick to follow his own advice.

Meanwhile, 911 calls kept feeding dispatchers fresh

information — and fresh worries. All 911 calls, except those from the larger cities of Aiken and North Augusta, were routed through a single office.

Within the first hour, so many were coming in that callers heard nothing but the fruitless beep-beep-beep of busy signals. Those that got through were assured that help was on the way — but not immediately.

First responders were encountering a poisonous cloud that was sweeping across the village. They couldn't get in any easier than residents and mill employees could get out.

"Yes, ma'am," an unidentified caller told a dispatcher. "A train derailment in Graniteville, there's something blowing off all over the town down here. I'm fixing to go down there and see. It's low to the ground, it's a fog, and it's everywhere."

A female caller on Harden Street reported a strong odor coming from the crash. But more disturbing was the man running down the sidewalk hollering for help.

An unidentified woman called, trying to check on her husband who was working at Woodhead. The last she had heard from him, he had told her the people in the plant couldn't breathe. She wanted to know if anyone was available to go look for him.

"We can't get in there right now," the dispatcher told her.

"Don't ya'll have ventilation or anything?" she asked.

All the dispatcher could offer was, "We're doing the best we can. I'm not trying to upset you. I'm just telling you the truth."

CHIEF PHIL NAPIER, GVW FIRE DEPARTMENT

AS A FIRST RESPONDER in a small community, Philip Napier Sr. was used to getting up at odd hours of the night. He had helped found the Graniteville-Vaucluse-Warrenville Volunteer Fire Department back in 1972, when he had gone door to door requesting $10 donations to buy the department's first truck.

He had served as fire chief since 1981. Since those earliest days, house fires, automobile accidents, even train wrecks had called him from his sleep.

Graniteville had suffered just such a tragedy seven weeks before, when a car carrying five Avondale Mills' employees pulled in front of a Norfolk Southern train at the intersection of Canal Street and Ascauga Lake Road.

The driver and four passengers died at the scene. Mourners laid wreaths and flowers beside the tracks. The Chief and his men were still learning to cope with what they'd seen.

Now, on the morning of January 6, Chief Napier's pager woke him at 2:39 a.m.

ATTENTION DISTRICT 3 GVW FIRE DEPT.

Initial reports indicated a train had derailed and struck a building on Hickman Street, a short distance from the Graniteville-Vaucluse-Warrenville fire station, and less than half a mile from the devastating wreck of two months before.

Oh, no. Not again.

Standard operating procedure for an emergency of this sort required members of the volunteer fire department to report to the station house on Main Street and stand by until the situation was assessed.

Chief Napier jumped in his truck and was on his way down Marshall Street to join his men when a voice he knew screamed out of the radio, "I can't breathe! I can't breathe! I need help!"

The accident was not yet in sight and one of his men was already in trouble. Rattled by the cries, Chief Napier ordered all units to clear the area. He would approach the firehouse on his own and try to get a grip on what was happening. He could always call for help once he knew what was going on.

Chief Napier continued down the steep slope of Marshall Street, passing the Gregg Plant on his left, unaware he had just entered the heart of the accident zone.

As he turned right onto Canal, he saw a man standing on the tracks across from the Masonic Shopping Center. A second man was sprawled across the rails. Fog wreathed them both, scudding along the heavy gravel embankments.

The Chief rolled down his window.

"We've had a head-on collision with a train," the man who was still on his feet gasped. "We've got a chemical leak. I can't breathe."

With that, he collapsed.

That's when the chemical cloud rolled over Chief Napier's truck. Chlorine struck him in the face and he choked, feeling as though his throat had been cut. Somehow, before his memory blanked, he managed to make a U-turn and step on the gas.

He came to his senses on the high ground at U.S. Highway 1 and the New Hope Crossing, with no idea how he had gotten there. The chlorine cloud remained coiled in the valley below him.

NORFOLK SOUTHERN

OFFICIALS AT NORFOLK SOUTHERN were aware of the accident within minutes of the crash. Engineer Seeling suffered superficial cuts and bruises, but he and his conductor were able to radio their Greenville dispatcher and let him know what had happened before they escaped the wreckage. They reported they were barely injured, but were having trouble breathing. They exited the train together.

It was not the initial collision that overwhelmed them. It was the chlorine that followed them down the tracks as they walked north toward Masonic Center, where Chief Napier first encountered them.

Norfolk Southern had faced disaster before. In 2002, a derailment in Tennessee spilled toxic materials, requiring an evacuation of nearby homes. But, there had been no deaths or injuries.

On the whole, the company was proud of its safety record. It had received the Harriman Award for employee safety for 15 consecutive years.

Now, facing a spill of unknown magnitude, the company worked quickly to contain the damage. Officials contacted experienced contractors who could rush to Graniteville to get the immediate situation under control and perform the subsequent cleanup.

Hulcher Services, Inc., was called to move wrecked rail cars and repair tracks, as was R.J. Corman Railroad Company, LLC. The Center for Toxicology and Environmental Health came to help monitor air quality. Hepaco, Inc., which specialized in hazardous materials cleanup, was asked to deal with whatever might be leaking, be it chlorine, cresol or sodium hydroxide.

When the crews were fully assembled, more than 450 men and women assembled by Norfolk Southern would offer their skills to supplement local agencies in dealing with the spill.

MIKE LAMBERT

MIKE LAMBERT WAS STANDING on the back of a finishing frame in the Gregg Plant when he noticed a faint whiff of bleach in the air. He thought nothing of it. Third shift was already not going well. The phones that made interdepartment communication possible had just gone dead. Someone had probably gotten snagged in the night's bad luck and spilled something in a room nearby. It wouldn't be the first time.

But as the odor grew thicker, Mike, a 16-year veteran of the Graniteville mills, became concerned. He walked to the nearest exit and looked out. As he passed the canteen, he glanced at the wall clock: 2:58 a.m.

The air outside was sharp as needles. Mike jerked his head back in and ran for a supervisor. There were 12 to 14 other men and women working the third shift in his second-floor department. His only thought was to get them all out.

He shut off the air conditioning system so more fumes wouldn't circulate through the plant and started making a circle, shooing people out as he went. He had never executed a real evacuation before, only trials, but right then he was glad for the practice.

As he neared an exit, Mike spotted two men lying on the ground outside. The first sat up as he approached, but the second wasn't going anywhere without help.

Mike recognized his friend Ben Cochran, who suffered from chronic asthma. Ben's eyes were scarlet and watering. He was foaming at the mouth. Mike had seen an asthma attack before, but never anything like this.

Mike's first thought was, *He's not gonna make it. Whatever this stuff is, it's killing him.*

Mike called for help. A co-worker, Curtis, came to help lift Ben by the armpits and drag him into a nearby lab. Once there, Mike handed Ben over to his co-workers and told them to take him to the hospital as quick as they could. Mike wanted to circle the department one last time to make sure no one was left behind.

By the time the circuit was complete, Mike began to wonder if he was going to make it out himself. He was coughing hard. His eyes were flooded with tears.

He made it outside and crossed the parking lot to unlock the main gates on Marshall Street. People escaping from the plant had to be able to get out. Rescuers had to be able to get in.

"C'mon, Curtis," he said. "Let's get out of here!"

Mike stripped off his outer shirt and gave it to Curtis to cover his face. The two of them climbed into Mike's truck and headed out.

If Mike had turned right, he would have gone up the hill of Marshall Street, and from there to Ascauga Lake Road, and safety.

But he didn't.

He went straight, down Leitner Street Extension. He didn't know there was a train derailment at the bottom of a hill, with a tanker car spewing death into the air.

AIKEN COUNTY SHERIFF MICHAEL HUNT

WHEN MICHAEL HUNT was a boy, Horse Creek Valley was still rural enough to depend on the rawest of recruits to staff its volunteer fire departments. Young men were expected to pull their weight in those days.

Hunt joined his local department when he was just 15. Every time an alarm summoned him and his fellow firefighters out of school to face a blaze, he felt a thrill go through him that told him he was meant to become a lifetime first responder.

Hunt grew up to become Aiken County Sheriff. Now, at 43, he was nothing if not a planner. His New Year's resolution the week before had been to continue building and strengthening relationships between his department and other law enforcement agencies throughout the state — a promise he had kept from the moment he had been sworn into office two years before.

A few hours into January 6, Sheriff Hunt would give thanks that his partnership building had not been neglected. Before the week was over, he and his county would need all the help they could get.

The September 11, 2001, terrorist attacks four years before had left law enforcement officials with a new wrinkle to consider whenever a major disaster struck: Was this an accident, or was it a deliberate act of terrorism?

Sheriff Hunt's pager told him of a train derailment accompanied by a chemical spill in downtown Graniteville, but that was all. He needed more information right away.

He called his dispatcher and asked if the wreck had occurred at a switch. Yes, he was told — right at the Hickman crossing.

Sheriff Hunt knew the switches along the Graniteville tracks were all manual. Anyone with the will and the know-how could tamper with one. He would have to assume the accident was an act of sabotage until he could prove otherwise.

Before he left his home on Laurel Drive, Sheriff Hunt woke his wife, Tonya, and asked her to monitor the television and stay off the phone.

He wanted her prepared if she and their son, Michael Jr., had to leave the house suddenly. The Sheriff had no proof, but his gut instinct told him the cloud spilling into the air a bare mile away was chlorine. He turned off his home's ventilation system, just in case the chemical should make it as far as Laurel Drive.

Then, he called Captain Paul Grant with the South Carolina Law Enforcement Division in Columbia. SLED implements the Homeland Security plan for the state of South Carolina. The agency could dispatch manpower and equipment with speed, should they be needed.

"I'll meet you at the staging area quick as I can," Sheriff Hunt told Captain Grant.

LAMAR LEDFORD

ABSORBED IN THE MONOTONY of his work, and the rhythmic hissing of the Bespoke's pneumatic pumps, Lamar didn't hear the crash. But he noticed its effects only minutes after it happened.

The air inside the plant simmered with the throat-stinging quality of a laundry kettle, until Lamar couldn't help but cough.

Huh, he thought, getting up to investigate. *Someone must have spilled some bleach. Or maybe there's been some sort of leak in the plant.*

The air quality worsened as he walked towards the door that separated the Bespoke room from the rest of the plant. Within a few steps, he was gasping for breath. It was a leak for sure. But where, and from what?

He had just broached his office door when two friends,

Junior and Coon, came pelting down the stairs that led to the mixing room above. They were choking and coughing as hard as Lamar was.

"What the f--- is this?"one friend said.

"It's upstairs, too?" asked Lamar.

"Jesus, it's getting worse!"

The only thing to do was get out, and get out fast. Because the men had been trained for emergencies, they bolted for their assigned fire exits.

Lamar's isolated office meant his route was different from the others. He had to go down a flight of stairs into the chemical warehouse and out onto a loading dock. He separated from his friends, silently wishing them luck.

But he wasn't running to safety. He was running into a suffocating cloud of chlorine gas.

CHIEF NAPIER

PHIL NAPIER'S CONSCIENCE gnawed at him. If he could have taken the two stricken men with him, he would have. But his training as a first responder had taught him he could be a victim or a survivor. A responder can't help a victim if he is a victim himself.

The Chief got back on the radio — much to the relief of his men, who were beginning to believe he was injured or dead — and started calling for HAZMAT teams from Aiken, Westinghouse Savannah River Site, and adjoining Richmond County and Fort Gordon, Georgia.

He had a major incident on his hands, an incident that had the potential to kill a lot of people. From what he had experienced down on the tracks, he knew an evacuation would be required. No one in Graniteville had ever dealt with a disaster of this magnitude before.

Once he was certain multiple HAZMAT teams were on the way, Chief Napier called home and told his 21-year-old daughter, Rebecca, to get her mother in the car and get out — now.

"Get in the car and go towards North Augusta," he told her. "Don't stop. Just drive. Now!"

He made a second call to his brother Ricky and asked him to go and get their mother, who lived on Hard Street, a bare 300 yards from the crash site.

He would later learn his mother had thought to put a cloth over her face, which may have saved her life. The cloth left a white bleach stain on the upholstery of Ricky's truck.

With his family on their way to safety, Chief Napier started calling other fire departments in the area to request mutual aid. A responder at the Bath Fire Department informed him he had a list of what chemicals were on the train and the order in which the cars had traveled before the derailment.

Three pressurized tank cars of chlorine gas, one car of sodium hydroxide and one car of cresol might have breached. The rail cars were jumbled in a pile with clouds of vapor rolling from them. There was no way to tell if one or all of the tanks were leaking.

Chief Napier reached for his Hazardous Material Response Guidebook. Chlorine. Not good. A minimum one-mile radius evacuation was required — maybe more.

That's when he realized victims closest to the crash were not waiting for a formal evacuation. People were pouring out of neighborhoods like ants kicked from a hill. Many were in serious respiratory distress. A handful literally foamed at the mouth, suffering the effects of chlorine inhalation.

Chief Napier directed those he could to Aiken Regional Medical Centers while he used his radio to request a decontamination site at the University of South Carolina Aiken. The university was located directly across the street from the hospital.

The Chief reasoned the injured could be moved from one site to the other with speed, depending upon how badly they were hurt.

A second decontamination site went up at Midland Valley High School.

Meanwhile, Graniteville-Vaucluse-Warrenville Station Two began to assist residents on the opposite end of Graniteville, where weeping, gasping people were attempting to escape up Ascauga Lake Road. They directed those who could make it to the nearest hospital.

Those who could not immediately move, or who needed an ambulance, were kept at the station until transportation arrived. More than 60 would find sanctuary there before the day was out.

MIKE LAMBERT

AS MIKE LAMBERT'S TRUCK sped downhill toward Woodhead, the air pressing against his windshield turned thicker and more noxious. He couldn't see anything but a slimy, green fog that reminded him of the scum in a stagnant fishpond.

"We aren't gonna make it out this way," he told Curtis. "We gotta get out of here."

Curtis evidently agreed. He was praying in a high, frightened voice. "Oh, Lord. Oh, Jesus. Oh, Lord."

Mike stopped the truck and turned it around blind in the road. He thought from the angle of the roadway that he must be across from the Woodhead Division, but he couldn't be certain.

He couldn't see the plant. He couldn't see the railroad tracks. He couldn't see anything but green.

He got the truck turned around without hitting anything. Straightened the wheel. And groaned as the truck gagged and died.

That's it, Mike thought. *This is where they're gonna find us dead.*

Resigned, he leaned his seat back and waited for God to claim him. He could think of nothing else to do.

REGINA READY

WHEN REGINA READY was growing up in Horse Creek Valley, hanging out in the Hardee's parking lot in Clearwater was the coolest thing to do. That's where she met a quiet, dark-haired young man with kind eyes, who already had a job stacking cloth in the gray room of the Gregg Plant.

Regina Ready and Ben Cochran clicked. They'd been together ever since, sharing their Langley home with their daughter, Dana, 13, and a passel of pampered Persians and Pomeranians.

On the morning of January 6, Regina was wakened by a call at 3 a.m. An employee at Gregg Plant told her there had been an accident. Ben was suffering an acute asthma attack that had been triggered when he breathed in a hazardous chemical. An ambulance was on the way.

Regina was worried, but not unduly so. Ben had been diagnosed with adult onset asthma in his early 30s. This was not his first attack on the job. She thought he would go to the hospital, endure a breathing treatment, and be home by dinnertime.

She didn't know at the time a serious accident had occurred, leaving nine people dead and hundreds injured.

She learned it soon enough. Call after call came in, giving her updates on Ben's progress. The ambulance had not come. One of Ben's co-workers had decided the only way to get him out alive was to put him in a truck and try for Doctors Hospital in Augusta. Someone would call her when he got there.

Regina turned on the television. The preliminary footage she saw spurred her to call her brother, who lived across the street, and ask him to come stay with Dana while she drove to Doctors Hospital to check on Ben.

She left Dana sleeping. There was no need to frighten her before Regina saw for herself how bad things were.

Ben arrived at the hospital at 4:30 a.m. Regina came in close behind him, but she was not allowed to see him for more than an hour. When she did, she was truly frightened for the first time.

Ben was white as an egg. Tubes ran into his wrists and into one leg. He was on a respirator, which wheezed in the quiet of the room. She was not allowed to touch him or talk to him. Doctors had him deeply sedated and wanted him to stay that way.

An ordinary asthma attack was dangerous. But Ben had suffered an attack and breathed in chlorine besides. His lungs were burned. Regina knew full well he might die without ever waking.

A calm, practical woman who had learned her steadiness through parenting and teaching middle school students, Regina allowed herself to be afraid, and then put her terror aside. Their family had to be notified of the accident, and in a few hours, Dana would waken, expecting to see her father at breakfast.

Regina had to be calm by then, for their daughter's sake.

LIZ PULVER, AIKEN COUNTY HAZMAT

LIEUTENANT LIZ PULVER pulled on her cargo pants, polo shirt and steel-toed boots with an edginess that wasn't like her. Twenty years in the Naval Reserve and an equal time spent in emergency response had left her with an instinct she couldn't explain.

The Maine native, who had once stood by for the Exxon Valdez disaster and who now served as a training and industrial relations officer with the Aiken HAZMAT Team, had a feeling in the pit of her stomach that this was no ordinary spill. This was a big one, and it was going to be bad.

Her pager instructed her to meet her team in the Kroger parking lot on Aiken's south side. Liz pulled in just ahead of her chief, Don Turno. She turned her head as she parked her car and saw the HAZMAT team from Westinghouse Savannah River Site pass by, headed for the other side of town.

A communications error had sent the Aiken team to the wrong staging area.

By the time the mix-up was sorted out and the team assembled at the forward staging area of Honda Cars of Aiken on U.S. Highway 1, Aiken HAZMAT was down to nine members.

More than 30 more were working the emergency through their primary jobs as firefighters, emergency medical technicians, or other first responder personnel. The chief and one other team member would report to command. That left seven to perform any missions that might be demanded of them.

It was not a large force, by any means. But Liz and her teammates had responded to hazardous chemical spills before. They had years of experience between them. She had confidence they could handle themselves in an emergency, no matter what the situation required.

FUSION, UNIFIED COMMAND

Forward Staging Area, Honda Cars of Aiken

BY THE TIME SHERIFF HUNT was en route to the staging area, 911 dispatchers were drowning in emergency calls. The Sheriff ordered all off-duty dispatchers recalled to help deal with the overload. Then he got on his cell phone and called Commander Wallace Owens to activate the Special Weapons and Tactics team, just in case Aiken County really had experienced a terrorist act.

Sheriff's Office personnel were already moving to shut down all access points leading in and out of Graniteville, including the four major roads at Ascauga Lake, Trollyline, New Hope Crossing and Ergle Street Extension. They would assist victims escaping the spill and prevent innocent bystanders from blundering into the cloud.

This was accomplished in a matter of minutes. As Sheriff Hunt had known, planning ahead paid off. When he reached the staging area, the Sheriff met with Chief Napier at once. The Chief, coughing and visibly shaken, but in control of himself, recounted a strong odor of chlorine at the accident site.

As other emergency personnel began to crowd in—Aiken County Emergency Services Director Rick Powell, Aiken

County Emergency Preparedness Coordinator David Ruth, Captain Grant of SLED, and various HAZMAT teams — updated information was relayed to them.

"This is bad, guys," Chief Napier told them. "It's major."

He gulped Gatorade as he spoke, trying to ease the rasp in his chest. He needed to go to a hospital to be evaluated, but he wouldn't. He couldn't leave his men when they and the people of his village were in such dire straights.

One man could not make all of the decisions in such a widespread emergency. A unified command developed, with Chief Napier in charge of fire control and HAZMAT operations and Sheriff Hunt in charge of law enforcement and security.

The South Carolina Department of Health and Environmental Control and the Environmental Protection Agency would oversee health and environmental concerns, and the National Transportation Safety Board and the Federal Bureau of Investigation took charge of the wreck investigation.

Dozens of other incident leaders were also involved as 18 agencies came on the scene to help in that first day.

Chief Napier asked Chief Howard Willis of the Augusta Emergency Management Agency and HAZMAT specialist Rudy Dinkins to take charge of the HAZMAT operation. He asked other HAZMAT personnel, including Aiken HAZMAT, to send in teams to reconnoiter the area around the accident.

Yet another team was needed to go into the Stevens Steam Plant and shut down the boilers. If victims were found in need of rescue, they would take priority.

Decisions were made rapid-fire. Command agreed the staging area was probably too close to the accident and should relocate as soon as possible.

Aiken HAZMAT Chief Don Turno — who had already volunteered his team for the reconnaissance mission — recommended the old Kmart parking lot on Richland Avenue. The area was large enough to accommodate incoming teams, and also low enough to contain the inevitable run-off of an active decontamination site.

Meanwhile, David Ruth moved to activate a reverse 911-call system that would instruct residents within a two-mile radius to shelter in place and turn off the ventilation systems to their homes.

It was better for those already within shelter to stay put, rather than risk driving into the spill.

MIKE LAMBERT

MIKE RESTED in a swirling green fog. The air in the cab was not getting any cleaner. On impulse, he returned his seat to the upright position and turned the key in the truck's ignition.

The engine revved to life. Mike stepped on the gas and tore up the hill, hoping there was nothing standing in his way. A head-on collision was all he needed, now that he was leaving the poisonous green cloud behind him. Streamers of fog waved from his truck antennae like evil little banners.

The next thing he knew, he had reached the roadblock at Bettis Academy and Ascauga Lake Road. An emergency medical technician helped him from the truck and immediately gave him oxygen. Another looked after Curtis.

The adrenaline high that had fueled Mike Lambert from the moment he had first smelled bleach finally gave out. He sagged against his rescuers, vaguely aware he was being transported to

GVW Station Two, where he was treated until an ambulance was available to take him to University Hospital in Augusta.

He saw flashes of lights. Flashes of people's faces. But nothing made sense. Mike Lambert closed his eyes and drifted away into the dark.

LIZ PULVER

THE REMAINING SEVEN MEMBERS of the Aiken HAZMAT team boarded HM1, a bright red truck that served as their command center on the job. Not yet certain what they were facing, they drove up the Aiken-Augusta Highway and turned onto Canal Street, where they intended to place book-sized monitors to detect chlorine levels in the air.

"We must be getting close," Liz protested, "shouldn't we finish suiting up?"

The team had no idea how close they already were. Liz looked out the window and saw a greenish yellow cloud floating by the glass. She and other team members began pounding on the truck bulkhead, shouting at the driver to turn around.

By the time he complied, Liz's throat stung. She covered her mouth with her coat and coughed, wondering how much chlorine she and her team had just inhaled.

HM1 stopped at 304 Canal Street long enough to place a single monitor near the wreck. Voices crackled on the radio, but nothing coherent came through.

As they drove narrow back roads to reach the Ergle Street Extension, Liz coughed until her throat was raw. Her captain made the decision to send her farther up the hill to the intersection of Ascauga Lake Road and Bettis Academy. There the original roadblock had been expanded to a medical staging area to assist evacuees in respiratory distress.

The intersection was clogged with people. Those in the worst shape were loaded onto ambulances for transport to a hospital. Those who could stand were ordered to strip down so they could be sprayed with water from fire hydrants to remove the worst of the chlorine. Once decontaminated, they were given blankets and their personal effects were packed into clear plastic bags.

Liz stood back. She was still coughing, but she was on her feet, which was more than most of the victims around her could manage. Once an emergency medical technician had checked her out and put her on oxygen for a precautionary 15 minutes, she found a commanding officer and volunteered her services.

She was out of the direct action, but she could still be of use.

LAMAR LEDFORD

LAMAR HIT THE LOADING DOCK and knew in one breath he couldn't stay outside. A green haze floated along the ground. Clumps of gas clung in yellow halos around the security lights.

Lamar turned to go back inside, but he was too winded to try to make it back up the stairs. He chose an office instead. He found his buddy Patrick working alone, where the first reek of chlorine was just beginning to slip into the room.

Patrick told him the phones within the plant were no longer functioning, but Lamar barely heard him. He propped a wastebasket on the desk and heaved streamers of clear mucus into it. He couldn't stop coughing.

Patrick told him to stay put. He would go see what was happening outside.

Pulling his shirt over his face, he made his way out into the plant, while Lamar, his choking temporarily eased, sat down in a chair and clamped a wad of tissue over his nose and mouth.

He had never been one to watch the clock at work before, but Lamar kept a watering eye on one now.

Watching the minutes tick away, he thought of Patrick's wife and three small children, and prayed, "God, if you have to take one of us, don't let it be Patrick."

MARK BROOME

MARK BROOME WAS ABOUT to make a patch. At every 2000 yards of cloth that came through his machine, he would snip out a square, take it to the shade room, and slice it into three pieces, where it would be compared to swatches to make sure the dyed cloth was turning out the correct color.

He noticed the faint odor of Clorox as he crossed behind his machine, but it wasn't strong enough to alarm him. Only when he was in the shade room, hemming the patch as he'd been taught, did he realize the smell was getting stronger by the second. It was stronger still when he stepped back inside the main plant.

Mark — 18, tall, dark haired and still outgrowing the gawkiness of adolescence — had worked in the Gregg Plant for only three months, but he knew there was an alarming number of potential hazards lurking in the plant's chemical basement.

Maybe one of the basement tanks had sprung a leak. He saw his co-workers shutting down their machines and hitting the doors, and he decided: He was getting out. He put a piece of cloth over his face and crossed the parking lot to his white Ford Taurus.

Mark chose his usual route home, down Marshall Street and right onto Canal. So much fog was drifting across the road that he couldn't see where he was going, but the smell of bleach spurred him on. He didn't know that one of the derailed cars from the train had sliced through a live oak, which was now — like parts of the train itself — blocking the two-lane road ahead.

When he hit it, he drove straight into the clutch of branches. One punched through the top of his windshield. His air bag deployed, sloughing skin from his right arm. His seatbelt jerked him up short as the roof of his car crunched downward.

Mark lay in his seat, stunned. The tree had completely engulfed his car. He struggled to open his door, but it was stuck tight.

He learned later that had he opened the door and tried to run for it, he wouldn't have crossed 30 feet of roadway before he collapsed and died.

He was sitting on top of the wreck, close enough to see the wink of lights from the train and hear the clanging of the crossing bell. White leaves pressed against his windshield like the innards of a monster had swallowed him whole.

Mark had never been the sort of angst-ridden teen who brooded over the prospect of his own death, but he considered it now. Funny, but this was not what he'd thought would happen to him.

Maybe a car accident, yes. He'd been in more than one collision, at one point ricocheting off the side of a truck at more than 100 miles per hour. But stuck in a tree, surrounded by a poisonous cloud that was burning his throat and eyes and thickening the saliva in his mouth? This sort of death was surreal.

This is the way I'm going to die. I don't want to die.

Mark loosened his seatbelt and crawled into the back seat.

Not realizing that chlorine would sink to the lowest level it could find, he crouched low, hoping the lethal vapors would float over him.

He watched the blink of the red lights through the black shadows of the leaves across his windshield and listened to the clang of the bell. His nose was running and his mouth felt as though it was full of hot motor oil. It hurt to swallow.

He had never been so terrified in his life.

ED SCHULER, AIKEN COUNTY HAZMAT

HM1 PARKED AT THE INTERSECTION of the Ergle Street Extension and Ascauga Lake Road. Thanks to the cloud that had engulfed their truck, the Aiken HAZMAT team now knew the wreck was close to where they had entered Canal Street, though they still had not laid eyes on the worst of it.

Lieutenant Ed Schuler, a certified hazardous materials manager and the technical and community relations officer for the Aiken team, suited up and prepared to walk back with a partner, Greg Bailey.

The hill leading down to the tracks was foggy and dark. No wind stirred the listless trees. There was no way to tell if the vapor scudding off Ed's mask was chemical, or merely the drift of natural moisture rising from the canal and Horse Creek.

The personal locator flashers attached to Ed's suit pulsed fierce yellow light through the gloom.

Ed kept his respirator off until he reached the canal at the bottom of the slope. He and Greg each had an hour's worth of bottled air, but that was an optimistic estimate.

They had just walked a mile down the hill, but they still

had a mile to walk up again. In between, there was no telling what they would find. Exertion would cut the air available to them by as much as twenty minutes.

Ed turned on his air. The rasp of his respirator echoed in his ears. As he and Greg walked down Canal Street toward the center of town, a sports utility vehicle rolled up beside them.

A man leaned out the window, "What's going on?"

"There's been a spill!" Ed yelled through his mask. "Get out!"

"My son is back there," the man said, indicating the road behind him. "Is he safe?"

"No," Ed said honestly. "He's not."

Before he or Greg could stop him, the man turned his vehicle around and tore off in the direction from which he'd come.

Ed watched him go, helpless. With any luck, the man would retrieve his son and escape.

The two men moved on. Walking lent sound to the otherwise eerie silence. A crossing bell clanged up ahead. A moment later, Ed saw the flashing red lights of the crossing behind what appeared to be a fallen tree.

As he came closer, he saw a live oak cut off at its woody knees, a white Ford Taurus tangled within the limbs.

Ed knew there was a high probability someone was trapped within the car. He moved forward as quickly as his suit would allow, climbing over limbs that poked and tore at him.

He reached the car and pounded on the glass. As he did so, he looked up and saw the black bulk of a rail car towering above him like a monolith.

This is it, Ed thought, awed. *This is ground zero. We're at the train.*

"Help me!" a voice screamed from inside the crushed Ford. "Help me!"

Ed Schuler had just found Mark Broome. He forgot about the train and began clambering over limbs, trying to reach a car door that wasn't crunched beyond hope of opening. None of the doors would budge.

"Roll down the window," he told the person inside the car, whom he still couldn't see. "It's okay, we're going to take care of you."

"I can't breathe!" the voice inside cried.

"Hold on," Ed assured. "We're going to get you out."

Ed got on his radio and called for a rescue team. He and Greg couldn't get the trapped victim out. They were already running out of air. But a second team could be on the scene within minutes. They materialized, it seemed to Ed, even faster than that.

Time is weird in an emergency, Ed thought, yielding the crash to the rescuers. *They got here in no time at all.*

Assured the victim in the car would soon be safe, Ed and Greg continued to reconnoiter the area. Overturned rail cars were piled up like a careless litter of cans.

One black tanker was split on one side, spilling vapor into the air. Ed reached for his radio and realized he had lost it in the grasping tangle of the tree. He would have to do without one until he reached HM1 again.

The tree limbs, the ground and the railroad tracks were all coated in thick white powder overlying a film of diesel fuel. At that time, intelligence on what the train was carrying was sparse.

The only thing Ed knew for sure was that one car was loaded with sodium hydroxide, a caustic which could appear in a white, granulated form. Ed wondered if that's what he was walking in. He hoped not.

He was picking his way through debris, trying to find a clear path, when his feet became tangled in the wreckage and he pitched forward, sliding down a steep embankment.

Ed fetched up against the bottom with a jolt. He got to his feet, shaken but unhurt. His suit was crusted in white powder.

You're all right. You're okay. Keep going.

He began searching amongst the cars for the placards that would tell him what was spilled on the ground, but he couldn't find them in the twisted wreckage. Instead, he noted the rail car numbers and had Greg call them in to HAZMAT command.

The streetlights over the jumble of cars glowed through the plume of vapors, turning the air a ghoulish orange. It seemed to Ed that the train was on fire.

Ed's mask began to vibrate with the alarm that warned him his cylinder pressure was getting low. It was time to go, and quick.

He and Greg didn't have enough air to walk back up the hill to where they had started. Their only option was to call for transport. As they neared the park directly across from the wreck, a woman in a car drove up and opened her door. She began to step out into the drifts of powder on the road when Ed yelled at her.

"You're right in the middle of a chemical spill!" he shouted. "Get out now!"

The startled woman obeyed. She turned her car around, with some difficulty, thanks to the debris, and headed back the way she'd come.

Ed and Greg met up with a county truck and climbed in the back, ready for the drive to the forward staging area for emergency decontamination procedures.

Once there, Ed stripped out of his suit and stood, in his

underwear, on the grass of Honda Cars of Aiken, while a colleague sprayed him down with freezing water from a fire hose.

There were no towels, so Ed grabbed another suit and climbed into it, soaking wet. He lived in it, the plastic hot and slick against his skin, until his next entry opportunity rolled around at daybreak.

LAMAR LEDFORD

FORTY-FIVE MINUTES PASSED one click at a time. Patrick had not returned, nor had anyone else passed by the office door. Lamar's breathing was worsening. He had to find a way to let potential rescuers know where he was.

He remembered his cell phone, then remembered with a groan that it was tucked into his jacket pocket, in his office up the stairs.

He had no choice. He had to go after it.

The mask of damp tissue pressed to his face didn't stop the chlorine. Lamar felt as though he was drinking bleach straight from a bottle. He could feel the poisonous vapor clinging to his tongue, slipping down his throat to choke him.

He reached his office, coughing violently once more, and stopped to rinse his face at a sink before he grabbed his cell phone.

Fingers shaking, he dialed 911.

"Help me," he wheezed into the phone, before the dispatcher answered. "Help. Help me."

"Nine-one-one."

"Help me," Lamar gasped. "I'm in... I'm in Gregg Plant."

"You're in Gregg Plant?" the female dispatcher confirmed.

"Yes."

"Sir, they are trying to get people inside those plants to help you, okay?"

"I can't breathe."

"Sir, I understand, they are trying to get people in there right now, okay?"

"I'm in the Bespoke room."

"You're in the what room?"

"Bespoke," Lamar said, "B-E-S-POKE."

"Are you there by yourself?"

"Yes," Lamar said, voice quavering, "I am."

"They are trying to get people in there to help ya'll, okay?"

"If I don't make it, please, tell my mamma I love her."

"Sir, they're coming as quick as they can, okay?"

"Please. Can I stay on the line with you? I don't want to be alone."

The dispatcher was busy. More calls were coming in all the time. But her calm, compassionate voice indicated she knew how frightened Lamar was. She did her best to accommodate him.

"Sir, hold on just a minute, okay?"

"Okay."

Lamar sat in his chair, panting for breath, listening to the 911 chatter filtering through his phone. In a moment, the dispatcher came back on the line.

"Sir?"

"Yes."

"Sir, I'm sorry, but they are trying to get that situation contained so they can get in there and help you, okay?"

"Oh, God," Lamar gasped, "I can't breathe."

"You're in the room by yourself?" the dispatcher asked again.

"Yes, I am."

"Do you have something maybe, you can cover... I don't know, do you have something you can cover your face with, maybe?"

"It's not helping," Lamar told her. "I tried."

"They are trying to get it contained," the dispatcher assured him. "The ambulances are coming in there to try to help, but it was doing the same thing to them, now. They are trying to get some masks and stuff so they can get in there to be sure to help ya'll. 'Cause they're not going to do you any good if they're passed out, too, you know?"

"I know," Lamar said with a strangled laugh. "I'm not complaining yet."

"No, no, I understand," the dispatcher said. "I know it's a scary situation."

"You can see a haze," Lamar told her.

"You can?"

"Yeah. Well, I can't open my eyes anymore."

"I'm still here with you, okay?"

"Thank you," Lamar said, heartfelt. He was overcome by coughing, but recovered. "What's your name?"

"My name is Janet."

"Hi," Lamar said cheerfully, as though introducing himself at a party. He was relieved he had someone to connect with in his time of need. "My name's Lamar."

"Lamar? Okay, Lamar."

"Oh, God," he said, the false cheer evaporating under fresh pain. "My lungs hurt so much."

"I know it seems like it's taking a long time, Lamar," the dispatcher said. "They're doing everything they can to try to get in to you."

"Oh, God. I don't know if I'm going to make it or not. His voice was becoming a liquid burble, like someone who was drowning one tablespoon of water at a time.

"You'll make it," the dispatcher insisted. "Just don't give up on me, okay?"

As the minutes passed, Lamar's breathing became more and more labored. His words to the dispatcher first roughened, then became garbled and thick, until they were unintelligible. Fragments of sentences were washed away in sobs.

Sixteen minutes into the call, Lamar lost himself. He began to scream into the phone.

"Help! Help! Help! No! Oh, God! Help!"

The screaming only stopped when Lamar ran out of air. He rested, panting. Then he looked down the length of his body. His dark shirt and jeans were bleaching pink and white before eyes.

Lamar gathered his strength. With a trembling voice, he asked the dispatcher to get his mother, Gail Ledford, on the line.

"Don't ask any questions, Mamma," he said when she picked up. "I wouldn't call if it wasn't serious."

For the next few minutes, Lamar spoke to his mother, telling her that he loved her. He asked to be cremated and have his ashes spread in front of the magnolia trees at the Boar's Head Pub in Savannah.

Lamar had been there only the week before, enjoying his favorite city and watching cargo freighters floating down the river. He hadn't dreamed at the time that he would be discussing his funeral arrangements with his mother only a few days later.

His mother, steady in her faith, never lost her composure. She prayed with him and read to him from the Bible. She told him that she loved him.

She stayed with him until 5 a.m., when the battery of Lamar's cell phone went dead.

It was all Lamar could do not to weep.

In spite of his best efforts to avoid it, he was going to die alone.

MARK BROOME

MARK BROOME DID NOT REALIZE two separate teams had come to his rescue. He would later learn that these men were a team comprised of Westinghouse Savannah River Site fire fighters Bill Elliott, Kevin Faircloth and Dwain Smith, and he would be grateful to them.

At that moment, Mark only knew he could no longer call out to whoever was outside the car. He reached forward and punched at the horn.

A disassociated voice told him to get down and cover his head. He crouched in the back seat while the team broke through the rear window. Arms reached in to the darkness to pull him out. Mark wiggled through the gap and felt an oxygen mask clapped to his face. He gulped in air, lightheaded with relief.

He barely remembered being stowed in the back of a truck for the trip to USC Aiken. Once in decontamination, the order to strip shocked him awake.

He pulled off his oddly faded jeans and shirt and found that his burgundy underwear had bleached white on his body.

Even the money in his wallet was contaminated.

Mark gave it all up without protest and rinsed down with cold water, shivering with goosebumps. He was still struggling to breathe, but he was alive.

For now, that was all he needed to know.

MURIEL COOK

MURIEL COOK WAKENED to a sound he interpreted as bricks cracking apart. He stayed in bed, listening. It was still dark outside.

Day was breaking before he ventured onto his front porch and got a whiff of metallic-tasting air. His good dog, Sadie, a square-chested mongrel who never strayed far from the porch, was nowhere in sight.

Oh no, Muriel thought. *We've been through this before.*

Muriel was thinking of the early 1950s, when an explosion at the Gregg Plant killed two men. He believed Gregg, or one of the other mills, must have gone up. If that was true, there was no telling what was tainting the air.

He stepped back into his tidy mobile home on Hester Lane and closed the door behind him, wondering where Sadie might be.

It wasn't until he turned on his television and saw the first of the news reports that Muriel realized he and his long-term companion — known affectionately in the community as Miss Morrall — were going to have to leave.

Hester Lane was so small it didn't appear on most maps, but the end of it butted up against a slope that led to Horse Creek. If chlorine followed the shape of the land, then the mobile home and the hardware store across from it were bound to take a hit as the cloud followed the creek bed.

Muriel began packing clothing and medicine for Miss Morrall, who had been incapacitated by a stroke some years before. He didn't think to pack for himself.

By 9:30 a.m., they were ready to leave — but Miss Morrall wasn't budging. She was home, surrounded by her things, where her beloved flowers waited in the yard for spring to call them to bloom. She took hold of her chair and refused to move.

"You have to go," Muriel told her. "I can't carry you, so you have to go."

She took some persuading, but at last Muriel got her out the door and down the steps. As he folded her into his truck, he looked around for Sadie, but he couldn't find the dog.

A stinging in his nose and on his lips convinced him he couldn't wait. He figured he would be home in a day or two and he could care for Sadie then.

But he hadn't made it to the end of Hester Lane before he was forced to reassess.

Two men wearing respirators were walking up the path. They stopped him and asked him if anyone was left on the street. Muriel wasn't certain if his neighbor was home or not. Then he pointed the nose of the truck toward Main Street, trying to concentrate on getting Miss Morrall to her eldest daughter's home in Stieffeltown.

He hoped he was wrong, but maybe they wouldn't make it home by tomorrow after all.

LAMAR LEDFORD

AS SILENT, LONELY MINUTES PASSED, Lamar's hazing mind alternated between optimism and fatalism. He figured others in greater need were being evacuated first, and that's why no one had come to get him.

He thought if the Graniteville Volunteer Fire Department had been in the path of the spill, surely they were in as bad a shape as he. He watched his friend, the clock, click off another round of 10-minute intervals and tried to think of a way to arrange himself so his body would appear dignified when he was found, but his imagination failed him. There was no dignity in such a death.

The clock ticked off another hour.

Lamar glanced up and saw the knob on his office door turning yellow.

My God. If it can do that to metal, what is this stuff doing to my lungs?

I can't just sit here and die. I've got to do something.

Emergency showers were scattered all over the Gregg Plant. The nearest was 30 yards from his office. That was a long way to stagger when a man couldn't draw a clear breath, but Lamar decided he had to try.

He grabbed at the shower's handle as he fell the last few steps and turned his face up into a rush of 51-degree water. The shock cleared his head, and he looked around to see what he could do next.

Ten feet away there was a computer monitor. If he stood beside it, he could see the length of the dye department. He was afraid if he sat on the floor he wouldn't be able to get up again, so he grabbed an overturned bucket and sat on that. He began a routine of showering every 10 minutes, then sitting down again to call for help.

His voice was raspy and raw. He had no voice left with which to shout. Lamar's pleas for his life were reduced to whispers.

MARK BROOME

DAVID HORNE SR., a first responder with the Clearwater Volunteer Fire Department, was helping to set up the decontamination center when his wife, Tammy, called. His stepson, Mark Broome, was trapped in his car on Canal Street, virtually atop the Graniteville train wreck.

David was staggered. He knew his stepson was working at Gregg. He had a nephew working the Stevens Steam Plant. But he had thought they both must be safely out by now.

As a first responder, David had seen people die at the scene of relatively minor car accidents. He couldn't imagine anyone surviving an extended period suspended in a cloud of chlorine.

Face it. If Mark is on top of the wreck, he's probably dead.

True as it was, David's mind couldn't grasp it. He had raised Mark for 14 years and considered him his own child. Numb with dread, he found his chief and asked for a ride back to the station house.

Once there, he met up with family members, who told him that Mark was on his way to Doctors Hospital in Augusta. Aiken Regional Medical Centers was packed. Patients were being diverted to any hospital that could take them.

Still in full bunker gear, David rode with his family to Augusta.

He was relieved — and astounded — to find Mark shaken, but safe. The young man was in the midst of chest X-rays, ultrasounds, and CT scans. His voice was raspy, and would thicken further within the next three days, as Mark developed bronchitis. But he was in far better shape than he had any right to be.

"I'm not a Christian man," David confessed to his family. "But God must have been with him. Mark's tough, but not even he should have survived that."

SHERIFF HUNT

MICHAEL HUNT THOUGHT that time seemed to fly. Media representatives were flooding in to the staging area as fast as first responders were.

The Sheriff decided access to the media could be an advantage. Television reporters could relay immediate instructions for Graniteville residents to shelter in place, since not all reverse 911 calls had gone through.

It was just as important, in the Sheriff's view, for the people of Aiken County to know that a major incident had occurred, but that their emergency responders were prepared to handle it. He especially wanted Graniteville residents tuning in to their televisions over the course of the day so they could receive instructions when an evacuation plan went into effect.

The Sheriff asked his public relations coordinator, Lieutenant Michael Frank, to prepare regular fact sheets for the media that would address what was happening in Graniteville, and what was being done to correct the most pressing problems as they arose.

A minimum of two live press conferences would be

staged every day of the disaster, until Graniteville was habitable again.

The remainder of the early morning hours was consumed by meetings with unified command, HAZMAT, and the Sheriff's own staff. His deputies were dressed out in personal protective gear consisting of a hooded suit and respirator designed to withstand biological or chemical attack.

The gear was part of the Homeland Security Plan — after 9/11, every deputy was required to carry it in their patrol cars. Sheriff Hunt was grateful for it now.

The suits allowed deputies to team up with firefighters to conduct rescues within the hot zone. Dozens of people attempting to leave the mills or their homes were rescued that way.

As the sun came up, a HAZMAT team went into the hot zone to videotape the crash. A SLED helicopter hovered overhead, assessing the situation and taking stills. Packets of photographs were distributed to first responders as they set up at the staging area, to give them an idea of how bad the accident really was.

Sheriff Hunt looked over the packet of stills in his hand and shook his head. A torn tanker was clearly visible, leaking a green cloud into the air. A white, granular material shrouded the ground and trees around the train.

Strange metal shapes that appeared to be barbells turned out to be the wheels of the train, torn off in the crash and scattered like bowling pins beside the Woodhead Division parking lot.

This was not going to be a one-day job. They had a lot of work to do.

Sheriff Hunt didn't want to think about how much worse the disaster could have been if it had happened mid-morning, when the mills were full of workers, downtown businesses were greeting customers, and Leavelle McCampbell Middle School and Byrd Elementary were full of children.

Sheriff Hunt's only son, Michael Jr., was a student at Leavelle. He would have been in class if the accident had happened six hours later than it had.

Sheriff Hunt shook off his sense of dread and straightened up. The problem in hand was bad enough. He couldn't let personal feelings or fears of what might have been interfere with his job.

An evacuation plan was the next vital step. He set deputies and public safety officers to work, gridding maps at the one- and two-mile radiuses from the crash, so the evacuation, when it came, would run quick and smooth.

LAMAR LEDFORD

THE CLOCK READ 7 A.M.

If this had been a normal morning, Lamar's shift would have ended in another hour, and he would have been going home.

No one's coming. If they do, they won't be in time.

It was time to go home. Now.

Lamar's truck was waiting for him in the parking lot on Marshall Street. If he took it slow and easy, he just might make it.

Twenty steps. Rest. Twenty steps. Rest.

Lamar's chest hurt. His lungs burned. His eyes teared and watered. He was afraid he would collapse at any moment, but he pushed himself to keep to his pattern.

Twenty steps. Rest. Twenty steps. Rest.

He glanced around him as he stumbled through the dying and finishing departments, afraid he would come across the bodies of his co-workers, but he saw none. He prayed most had escaped, even if he had not.

At the stairway, Lamar leaned hard on the railing to pull himself up. Something fragile in his left foot let go with a crunch. His awkward gait had snapped his fifth metatarsal.

As he staggered through the lot and found the door of his truck, Lamar thought with a panic that he might have left his keys in his office, but they were in his jeans pocket, where he usually kept them.

Shaky with relief, but still frightened, he cranked up the engine and drove down the hill of Marshall Street with his emergency flashers on. He wobbled down Horse Creek at 30 miles an hour, struggling to stay conscious and to keep his truck on the narrow road.

While on the phone with Janet, the 911 dispatcher, Lamar had heard the background chatter of relief efforts organizing at USC Aiken. He figured that was the best place to go.

At the Robert M. Bell Highway, Lamar finally found what he'd been looking for: a police roadblock. He stuck his head out the driver's side window and croaked, "Help me."

Boy, he thought, with amusement only slightly tempered by shock and relief. *Those officers sure do seem surprised to see me.*

They were. Lamar was the last man to get out of the Gregg Plant alive.

DONNIE WILLIAMS

HE WOKE IN THE NIGHT with no clear idea of what had startled him, but he wasn't concerned. As a Graniteville native who had lived in the neighborhood of Rocktown for the past 30 years, he was used to loud noises emanating from the tracks as the trains came through. He visited his bathroom and went back to bed.

But when he got up at daylight, Donnie had a feeling something wasn't quite right. He walked out into his yard and saw his neighbors' cars were all gone. His old red truck was the only vehicle left on the street.

The quiet of the morning pressed down in foggy gloom. There was nothing to hear but a faint skittering from a pine tree near the street. Donnie walked over to investigate and saw something he had never seen before: twelve squirrels, running nose to tail in a furry stream, circling the tree in a mad scramble, over and over and over again.

What in the world...?

Just then an ambulance drove up. Two men in HAZMAT gear jumped out. One of them grabbed Donnie by the arm.

"Get in the back!"

"Who in the hell are you talking to?" Donnie demanded. He thought someone on his street must have taken a bad turn in the night and called for help. "I haven't had a heart attack. I'm fine."

"Get in the back!" the man in the respirator insisted. "There's been a train wreck, a chemical leak. It's time to get out!"

Donnie was still protesting and trying to retrieve his arm from the stranger's grip when a car drove up. Donnie had breakfast with his parents every Tuesday and Thursday morning, and his father had arrived to fetch him.

The men in the ambulance gave up once they saw Donnie had another way out of the danger zone. They left him, and Donnie climbed into the car with his father. He still didn't know what to make of it all.

As the car neared Canal Street, Donnie understood all too well. He saw smoke spilling from a jumble of rail cars and blanched.

"No, Daddy, don't go that way. Turn around." Donnie Williams had worked in chemical factories before he retired. He didn't know what was spilling from those cars, but he knew it couldn't be good. "My god, Daddy, there's a tanker in the road."

The men in the ambulance hadn't mentioned that the train wreck was practically in Donnie William's back yard. He was only 450 feet from the crash.

Donnie went to his parents' house for breakfast, as he usually did, but by 5 p.m., their street was evacuated, too. Donnie went to a motel, while his parents went to relatives in North Augusta.

Before he reached his room, a pack of shouting children told him he had found the neighbors he had missed that morning. The motel was jam with displaced Graniteville residents.

Donnie got a beer and settled in with them to wait.

BOB DOWNING

BOB DIDN'T HEAR the crash from his home on Laurel Drive, but when the television footage began rolling in, he understood the implications better than most.

The son and grandson of Graniteville mill workers, Bob had worked in a mill weaving room as a teenager. He grew up to become a chemist for the South Carolina Department of Health and Environmental Control. Stricken with multiple sclerosis at 43, the man who had once written short stories and produced a music album was now confined to a wheelchair. But his mind still recalled a background rich in chemistry.

Bob knew what chlorine was. He knew exactly how dangerous the stuff could be.

Humans come in beneficial contact with chlorine every day. As a natural element, it's a component of sodium chloride: common table salt. As a widely used industrial chemical, chlorine is used to disinfect municipal drinking water supplies and figures prominently in the production of paper products, textiles, solvents and paints.

But chlorine has a more dangerous side.

"It's not good," Bob explained, "for oxygen-dependent life forms."

Exposure to as little as one part per million of gaseous chlorine in the air results in stinging, watering eyes and irritation of both the skin and the mucous membranes of the upper respiratory tract. This results in coughing, choking and a burning sensation in the throat. Concentrations greater than three parts per million can cause breathing difficulties, skin burns and eye corrosion. Prolonged exposure may lead to delayed lung edema and death.

Armies once used chlorine's more aggressive traits to their advantage. The Germans first used chlorine cylinders against the French at Ypres in 1915. The effects of the gas on the human body were so horrible the 1925 Geneva Protocol outlawed its use as a weapon.

First aid for acute exposure requires removing the victim from the contaminated area, removing clothing, washing the body in cold water, administering humidified oxygen and seeking immediate medical care.

There is no antidote for acute chlorine exposure. Prompt medical assistance may help, but there is no hard and fast guarantee of recovery.

Bob watched television updates of the disaster while his wife, Annette, packed clothes and rounded up the family dogs. They would evacuate to Bob's sister-in-law's home in Aiken, knowing the village they left behind would never be the same.

JOANNE LEOPARD

BETTY JOANNE LEOPARD FOLLOWED her usual routine the morning of the crash. She was already feeling under the weather, thanks to an upset stomach. She stayed in her mobile home, tucked out of sight in the sheltering woods on Swint Street, and played with Candy, her Maltese pup.

Mid-morning she turned on the news: "Stay in your home. Don't open doors or windows. Turn off any ventilation systems."

A train had derailed only a few blocks away, but Joanne had not heard it.

A moment later, Joanne's phone began to ring off the hook. Friends were checking in to make sure she was all right. Kyle, a friend and neighbor, knocked on her door before lunchtime.

"Joanne," he said, "there are so many roadblocks I couldn't drive up here, so I shot across the woods to see about you."

Joanne assured him she was all right. She had heard on the news that residents in the affected area could expect a visit from a police officer, who would instruct them to evacuate. That call hadn't come, so Joanne figured she must be safe.

She wasn't. She was in the hot zone, where she would stay for the next seven days.

ED SCHULER

AT DAYBREAK, Ed Schuler and teammates Andy Sharpe, Robin Ford and Bruce Hewett prepared to re-enter the hot zone. Avondale personnel would accompany them in order to shut down steam and electric services in the plants.

Ed and Andy took their mill representatives with them to Gregg, while Robin and Bruce went on to Woodhead.

Ed entered the plant from the loading dock. He had walked but a few feet into the main facility when he looked into an office and saw a man slumped in a chair.

Oh, man, Ed thought, pity tightening his throat. *He does not look good.*

This was a rescue operation as much as re-con, but Ed, a former emergency medical technician, knew even as he and Andy lifted the man from the chair to the floor this victim was beyond help. He was dead.

Ed tried to find vital signs anyway, but could find no pulse at throat or wrist. He saw a cell phone on the floor and picked it up. The family might want to claim it later.

Farther into the plant, the men found a second victim lying on the floor of a break room. The large man's skin was mottled and discolored. Again, Ed attempted to find vital signs, but there was no pulse. He lifted an eyelid to check for pupil dilation and found the eye socket full of blood.

Ed had served all his life as a first responder. He had seen death in accidents, in fires, and in natural disasters. This was the first time he had witnessed a chemical death. It was like nothing he had ever seen.

He couldn't have suffered long, Ed hoped. *He got a massive dose. He went down hard. Hard and fast.*

He kept telling himself that as he accompanied the Avondale representatives through the plant, turning off machinery.

Limited by their air supply, the men did not have time to check all of the plant, but they did what they could. Once outside, Ed tried to call in to command on his replacement radio, but he had no luck.

Communications within the valley were still scattered. He would have to return to command to report the deaths.

LAMAR LEDFORD

AN OFFICER TOLD LAMAR to turn off his truck. Another ran for an oxygen canister and to call for an ambulance. Attendants arrived in HAZMAT gear.

Lamar was grateful for the assistance, but he couldn't help thinking, *Where were you guys three hours ago?*

His contaminated clothing had to come off, then and there. He stripped down in the middle of the street, while commuters at a nearby convenience store stared.

Lamar ignored them and wrapped himself in the sheet an officer offered him. He climbed into the ambulance, longing to lie down, but the emergency service technician riding in the back with him asked him to sit up instead.

"Some of your co-workers didn't make it out," the technician told him.

Lamar shivered, wondering if one of the dead was his

buddy Patrick, who had gone for help.

The ambulance reached USC Aiken, where one of two decontamination centers had been erected to help those exposed to the chlorine cloud.

Lamar had been hoping for a hot shower. He could still feel a film of chlorine burning on his skin. What he got was more cold water trickling from a hosepipe inside a tent. He scrubbed down as best he could, then was led to a second tent, where a physician was conducting triage.

The physician asked Lamar where he had been when the spill occurred.

"Gregg Plant," Lamar replied. "I work there."

The physician nodded, turning to a second man awaiting treatment and repeating the question.

"I just wanted to see a train wreck," the man replied.

Lamar rolled his eyes.

LIZ PULVER

AS THE SUN CAME UP over the first day of the disaster, Bridgestone/Firestone South Carolina sent breakfast to the first responders at the medical staging area from its plant farther up Bettis Academy Road.

Liz Pulver took advantage of the gathering light to take notes she would later record in her HAZMAT log.

When firefighters were called back to command — now situated in the parking lot of an old Kmart on Richland Avenue in Aiken — Liz hooked a ride, hoping to catch up with her team.

She found HM1 parked across the street in front of a laser tag arcade, with teams of two dressing out to go back in to the hot zone.

Unable to wear a respirator because of her persistent cough, Liz helped other team members pull on chemical-resistant Saranax suits outfitted with self-contained breathing apparatuses. Each canister held approximately one hour of air — or 45 minutes under serious exertion.

Since Liz had left that morning, Greg and Ed had entered the hot zone twice and were preparing for a third.

Each time they exited, they had to undergo decontamination procedures and don a fresh suit. Liz helped them tug on three pairs of purple surgical gloves with a pair of heavy green chemical gloves pulled over that. She taped up their wrists and ankles and made sure their chemical boots held a snug fit.

Once the men were outfitted, they departed for Honda Cars of Aiken to receive their missions.

Liz, once again out of radio contact because of the fluctuating communications coming in and out of the valley, kept her frustration to herself and kept working.

She became the team scribe, taking notes of all she observed. She would have plenty to record before the day was over.

UNIFIED COMMAND

SHORTLY BEFORE NOON, South Carolina Governor Mark Sanford toured the crash site by helicopter. He told news crews he had seen at least one human body and several animal carcasses on the ground, and voiced fears more victims would be discovered inside residences closest to the wreck.

Not long after, he signed an executive order declaring a state of emergency in Aiken County.

Norfolk Southern, in the meantime, was taking steps to assist the people who would be displaced by the evacuation. An aid center was established at First Presbyterian Church in Aiken, where evacuees could request financial assistance for food, clothing, shelter and medicines.

"We are profoundly sorry," said Norfolk Southern spokesman Robin Chapman in a formal apology to the people of Graniteville. "We will do everything within our power to ease the pain that this has created for the residents of Aiken County."

Shelters were organized at First Baptist Church in Aiken, Midland Valley High School, South Aiken High School and USC Aiken to take in anyone who needed a place to stay until the emergency was over.

Hundreds—including families with small children—took advantage of the offer, while others sheltered with relatives, friends, or in hotel and motel rooms from Augusta to Aiken.

SHERIFF HUNT

A WIDE-SCALE MANDATORY EVACUATION was now under way, assisting those who had not already decided to leave the village on their own.

Graniteville was divided into 11 grid sections within a one-mile radius of the crash. Eleven law enforcement teams would enter those neighborhoods and encourage residents to leave.

Sheltering in place was no longer a viable option. A late afternoon rain would knock down chlorine vapors, but would encourage what was left of the cloud to hug the ground, where it could seep into basements and crawlspaces beneath homes.

Chlorine mixed with falling water became hydrochloric

acid — acid rain. The plant life in Graniteville was about to take a beating.

There was an additional problem. Most of the original release was dissipating, but chlorine was still trickling into the air from the fractured tanker. A second chlorine tanker that had been crumpled in the crash made another release a definite probability.

Before contractors hired by Norfolk Southern could go in, cap the leak, and remove the wreckage, residents in the hot zone had to be out of danger. No one wanted to expose them to a second dose of gas.

As if that wasn't enough, a fire had broken out at the Stevens Steam Plant. GVW volunteers were struggling to extinguish a blaze that had ignited in the coal-burning boilers.

The fire was eating its way up the coal chute towards the silo. If the silo went, Graniteville would be covered in a layer of thick black soot as well as remnants of the chlorine cloud, a complication they did not need.

As Sheriff Hunt had hoped, the evacuation, at least, was moving quick and smooth. More than 5,400 residents were evacuated in an hour and a half.

More good news, faint as it was, came when the Sheriff was certain the accident was truly that — an accident — and not a terrorist act. Photographs of the crash and interviews with survivors had convinced him human error was the cause of the spill — an opinion backed by the National Transportation Safety Board.

Someone had failed to re-set the manual switch at the Hickman Street crossing, the switch that would keep trains on the primary track and away from the siding. It was as simple as that.

In a way, that's even worse, Sheriff Hunt thought. *Who ever caused this will have to live with it for the rest of their lives.*

What a terrible burden for anyone to have to carry.

ED SCHULER

AFTER LUNCH, Ed and his teammates returned to Graniteville to complete the evacuation of Rocktown, a neighborhood that included the cluster of stone and wooden houses where Donnie Williams and his neighbors lived.

Ed was shocked at how many people were still in the area. He had thought everyone would have bolted when they heard the wreck come crunching through.

If a door was open, Ed and his men took advantage of the opportunity to investigate, praying like hell they wouldn't find any more victims. If a resident answered their knocks, they urged the person to leave.

Most did, but a dozen Graniteville residents declined. They cited debilitated family members, animal companions, or simple stubbornness as their reasons.

Ed could not force them to evacuate, but he did get a phone number for next of kin, hoping no one would have to use the information later. Graniteville had lost enough lives.

SHARON MCLAUGHLIN

ALTHOUGH SHE DID NOT encounter Ed Schuler personally, Sharon McLaughlin was one of the Graniteville residents who would have exasperated him.

The author and artist, who published the monthly newspaper *The Villager*, preferred handing over the number of her next of kin to evacuating the home she had grown up in on Horse Creek Road.

Sharon was unaware of the accident until 9:30 a.m. She was out on her porch, drinking orange juice and enjoying the sunshine, when she heard her phone ringing. She went inside and found 15 messages waiting for her.

Her brother-in-law, Joe, told her what had happened. He advised her to turn on the TV.

"It's a mess down there," he said.

Joe was right. Sharon could barely believe what she was seeing. She hurried outside to call her dogs.

Ginny, a rotund mutt who hadn't missed a meal since Sharon had rescued her, and President Albert Gore (Bert, for short), an enormous black lab mix with a white chest and a baying bark, came bounding up to her. They were ready to come in, which wasn't like them on such a fine, sunny day.

Sharon brought them in and closed off the porch. She saw no sign of her black cat, Max, but hoped he would turn up sooner or later. She kept an eye out for him as she turned off her heater and duct-taped her vents shut.

When the house was as secure as she could make it, Sharon called back the friends that had left messages earlier in the morning. "If the Red Cross comes knocking at your door, don't worry," one told her. "I sicced 'em on you when I didn't hear from you."

Sharon considered all day what she should do. She spoke to neighbors, who had left their chimney flu open the night before so they could build a fire in their fireplace.

Their house had filled with chlorine fumes, and they were feeling ill. Their dogs, which had spent the night outside in the yard, were listless and subdued. The neighbors packed up and left, taking their dogs with them. But before they went, they encouraged Sharon to come along, or at least to leave soon after.

Sharon didn't. She couldn't figure out how she would load two enormous dogs and a cat into her tiny car. Still, she thought about it.

She found a piece of rope that might serve as a harness in

handling Bert, who was almost as big as Sharon. A collar and leash alone wouldn't hold him. Even the rope seemed a flimsy bit of safety for such a rambunctious dog.

Just after lunch, Sharon looked out her window and saw Max sitting on the hill behind her house. She had thought him gone, especially after she saw television footage describing animals dropping dead around the crash site.

She ran outside and called him in. Max came leaping over the grass to her. Sharon shut the door behind him, grateful to have all her "children" safe in the house. She had few surviving family left to her. Her pets really were her "babies."

That was when something odd occurred to her.

Max had come running when she called. But there hadn't been another living thing moving in the yard. Not a bird. Not a squirrel. Not a stray cat or dog. The entire neighborhood was completely silent.

Sharon felt cold inside. Maybe leaving was the right thing to do, after all.

At 5:45 p.m., a police officer knocked on her door. Sharon spoke to him through the glass storm door.

"Lady," he said, "this is a mandatory evacuation."

"How long do I have to get out?" Sharon asked.

"You should have left hours ago," the officer said. "There's a dusk to dawn curfew in effect as of 6 p.m. It's a quarter till, now."

"I can't leave without my dogs and cat," Sharon said. "I can't take them with me all at once. I need to stay with them."

"You can't help them if you're dead," the officer observed. "You need to leave now."

Sharon noted that the officer, who was emphasizing her danger, was not wearing a respirator or any other kind of emergency gear. That made it harder to take him seriously.

If what he says is accurate, he's in a lot more trouble out there than I am in here, she thought.

"Maybe I can take them out one at a time," Sharon considered aloud. "What happens if I'm out a little while after the curfew?"

"You'll do jail time," the officer said shortly.

"I guess you just made my decision for me," Sharon said. "I can't leave them."

The officer was obviously exasperated. Sharon thought he was considering tucking this stubborn little old lady under his arm and chucking her in his patrol car. Instead he went and got a pad of paper and a pencil from his front seat.

"I can't force you to leave," he said. "But we'll need the name and number of next of kin, so we can inform them when we find you dead in the morning."

Sharon bristled at the "when." She knew the officer was trying to help her, but intimidation was the wrong tactic to take with a woman who had been stubbornly self-sufficient all of her life. She gave him the name and number of a cousin and shut the door.

Before he left, the officer tied a bit of crime scene tape to the wrought iron railing on her steps. She supposed that was so officers could find her house in the morning.

But she didn't see another in the flesh until she ran out of groceries the following week.

PAMELA HALL

PAMELA HALL DIDN'T have to have anyone ask her twice to get her family out of Graniteville. As soon as word came over the television a mandatory evacuation was underway, she packed up her mother, Rosalee, her nine-year old son, Latrell, and her nine-year-old nephew, Keon, and prepared to leave.

The family had spent the morning inside their home on Seastrunk Street, fending off thickening vapors by resting in their beds with their heads beneath blankets and towels clamped over their mouths.

Latrell suffered from asthma, and his breathing was becoming increasingly labored. All of the family was having difficulty as the afternoon progressed.

When a television reporter finally said it was time to leave, Pamela took him at his word and packed. She didn't take much. She didn't expect to be gone more than a day or two.

On the way out, Pamela went door to door, asking neighbors if they had a way to leave. Many residents on Seastrunk did not own cars. In minutes, Pamela had 12 people packed into her two-door vehicle, smushed in anywhere they could find a seat or a lap.

Police officers assisting with the evacuation noticed the overcrowding, but said nothing. That only confirmed Pamela's fears the spill was worse than she had initially believed.

As she drove away, she noticed the gray siding on the house wasn't the same color it had been the day before. It was lightening, right before her eyes.

LAMAR LEDFORD

IN THE EMERGENCY ROOM of Aiken County Regional Medical Centers, Lamar underwent X-rays on his chest and foot. Doctors told him the oxygen level in his blood was down to 64 percent.

Lamar wasn't stable yet, but his natural optimism had returned. He feared he might be connected to an oxygen canister for the rest of his life, but still managed to joke with the nurses and ask the doctor for a prescription for Scotch.

His mother, Gail, and his Aunt Nelle arrived soon after, looking for him. They had tired of waiting for word and had driven down to the roadblock at the Robert M. Bell Highway, where they were told that Lamar had already been transported to ARMC.

Lamar did not like the expression on his family's faces. They looked frightened, but he was glad to have them there. One woman stood on either side of him, holding his hands and supporting him through the violent coughing fits that struck every few minutes.

His throat was raw, burning as though a hot sickle was trying to cut its way out from the inside. The pain was so bad his eyes teared up at times, but he wasn't embarrassed.

Lamar was euphoric. Against all odds, he was alive.

DAY'S END

AS THE SUN SET behind a pall of storm-ridden clouds, Graniteville sat strangely silent and alone. No dogs barked. No birds sang. No villagers walked the streets. Abandoned vehicles littered the roads. The mills did not rumble their song of commerce.

Avondale had suspended operations at Gregg, Woodhead, Hickman, Swint, Townsend, Horse Creek, Warren, the Stevens Steam Plant and Sage Mill, as well as its Graniteville and Warrenville administrative offices.

Mills within the hot zone were incapacitated, their stock and machinery damaged by chlorine. Warrenville mills were not injured, but many were in the evacuation zone, and if they were not, their employees were.

AT 9 P.M. THE AIKEN HAZMAT TEAM stood down. Liz Pulver returned home to take a shower and rest before she had to return to command at 7:30 the next morning.

Tired as she was, she couldn't sleep. She had trained workers out of the Avondale plants for the past seven years. She realized she must have known the men who had died. She was thankful she hadn't seen their bodies. Her imagination gave her enough fodder to dream on as it was.

Try as she might, Willie Tyler, an Avondale employee who was not yet accounted for, would not leave her thoughts.

She remembered him as a strong, good-hearted man of faith who loved to sing. She had liked and respected him. She could not believe he was gone. She hoped he wasn't. But she believed that he was.

The only comfort Liz found was in a memory she had kept from that afternoon. While she was helping to outfit her teammates, three Avondale employees had tracked her down at HM1 to make sure she was okay.

Liz was deeply touched they had taken the trouble to find her. She had spent an emotional moment with them, there at the side of the road.

"Thanks for the training, Liz," one told her. "You don't realize how important that is until you have to face the real thing. You may have saved some lives today."

That one kind remark was the touchstone that would get Liz through the night.

An exhausted Ed Schuler returned to command glad he

was wearing his HAZMAT gear. Even through the chemical suit, his skin tingled and burned.

His voice was weak and there was a pronounced heaviness in his chest. He had no doubt that his suit had saved him from harm more than once that day. He could only imagine what condition he would be in without it.

Ed went through yet another decontamination before he attended a HAZMAT debriefing at command and headed home. He had less than six hours to rest before he would have to climb back into a suit, ready to return to the hot zone.

Much as he wanted to, Chief Napier found he could not work all night. But he couldn't sleep, either.

How can anyone lay down to sleep without worrying himself to death?

The Chief was frustrated. Seven weeks before, he had witnessed a train moving at more than 40 miles an hour down the Graniteville tracks. He had thought then, *That boy's going way too fast.*

Moments later, the alarm indicating a vehicle/train collision began to sound. Chief Napier had run to the crumpled car on the tracks beside the canal. There he had seen the expressions of fear on the five dead faces inside.

At that moment, he had known he had to do something to get the trains to slow down before they entered the village, especially during school hours and mill shift changes.

The Chief had done his best. He had appeared before the Aiken County Council and asked them to pass a resolution that would require Norfolk Southern to slow its trains within the village limits.

"What happens if a train loaded with chemicals — say, chlorine — comes through and wrecks?" he asked.

He was told that such a resolution was beyond the Council's

power. State or federal intervention was required to slow the trains.

The fact that Chief Napier's words had proved prophetic were no comfort to him, nor was the fact state officials had agreed to look into legislation that would require the trains to slow down.

Action had come too late to save eight lives. He firmly believed had Train 192 been traveling at 25 miles an hour instead of 41, it probably still would have crashed, and might even have derailed, but the disaster would not have been as bad as it was.

Still, there was nothing he could do about that now. He needed rest. Chief Napier caught a half an hour here and there, his body still ringing with an adrenaline buzz dampened only by sadness.

Graniteville was a small community. Chief Napier had known most of disaster victims personally. He knew their families and their friends. There was little he could do but mourn with them until the victims' bodies were recovered and decently laid to rest.

The day was winding to a close for Sheriff Hunt, too. Like Chief Napier, he was saddened by those lives lost in the spill.

Five of the victims were employees of Avondale Mills. Willie C. Shealey, 43, of Graniteville, and John Laird Jr., 24, of North Augusta, were found dead in the woods behind the Woodhead Plant, where they had tried to out run the chlorine cloud.

Fred (Rusty) Rushton, 41, of Warrenville, was discovered on a loading dock at the Stevens Steam Plant. Allen Frazier, 58, of Ridge Spring, had been located in an office of the Gregg Division, while Steven Bagby, 38, of Augusta, was found in the break room of the same plant.

Autopsies would show that the five men all died of chlorine poisoning.

Engineer Christopher Seeling, 28, of West Columbia, had been brought out of the hot zone alive, but he was pronounced dead a short time later at Aiken Regional Medical Centers. His cause of death was established as lactic acidosis, a build up of lactic acid in the blood caused by breathing chlorine.

Engineer Seeling's conductor, who had escaped the cloud in a pick up truck full of mill employees, was hospitalized, and would remain so for the foreseeable future.

Two other victims had been discovered during the evacuation. Joseph L. Stone, a young driver from Quebec, Canada, had been sleeping in his semi-truck near Woodhead Division when the cloud rolled over him.

He died of chlorine poisoning, as did Tony DeLoach, 56, who expired in his residence on Main Street as his family repeatedly called 911 for help. Mr. DeLoach's house was fatally close to the crash.

Sheriff Hunt caught an hour of sleep in his patrol car, then drove over to Aiken Department of Public Safety Station Three for a shower.

He needed to be awake and alert. Eighteen agencies had addressed the first day of the emergency, ranging from sheriff and public safety offices to Emergency Management Services to DHEC to the FBI. Many more would be on their way to Aiken to assist with the subsequent cleanup.

Another long day was about to begin.

DAY 2

JANUARY 7, 2005

NORFOLK SOUTHERN

WHILE FIRST RESPONDERS sought what rest they could, Norfolk Southern contractors worked through the night to remove 26 undamaged rail cars from the wreck site.

Like the firefighters, police officers and HAZMATers before them, the workers were forced to labor in protective gear and respirators that slowed their progress, but kept them safe from airborne pollutants. They relied on floodlights to illuminate the scene.

As Friday morning dawned, the contractors stopped work to allow rescue teams to search Woodhead and the surrounding woods for Willie Tyler, the Avondale employee who was still missing.

Meanwhile, Avondale Mills established a telephone calling-tree to account for all Gregg Plant employees, to ensure no one else who might be missing and overlooked.

The virulent green cloud that swept through the village had dispersed, but chlorine still remained in the air, thanks to the leaking tanker.

Teams from Westinghouse Savannah River Company, the South Carolina Department of Health and Environmental Control and the Environmental Protection Agency conducted air quality monitoring at the intersections of Aiken and Canal Streets, Holsenbeck and Main Streets, and the Masonic Shopping Center.

The highest reading they found registered at 1.5+ parts per million at Aiken and Canal, the intersection closest to the crash.

Chlorine levels of 10 parts per million are considered extremely harmful, but any concentration below one part per million is considered safe. Graniteville still had hours to go before its air was breathable again.

MURIEL COOK

The day after the accident, Miss Morrall developed breathing problems. She was transported to a veterinary hospital, where she would remain for the next six days, pining for her home.

Muriel Cook went to stay with a friend. He spent the week following the news in the papers and on TV. A self-employed handyman at the age of 61, there wasn't much else he could do. His tools were at home, and there was a roadblock of highway patrolmen between him and Hester Lane.

As much as his work, Muriel missed his kitchen. He missed cooking chicken and collards and sweet potatoes in the evenings. The food he bought at local restaurants was good, but it wasn't as satisfying as home.

As footage of the accident rolled across the television screen, Muriel took the fatalistic view that is so common to Horse Creek Valley. He had known Tony DeLoach when the man was only a boy. He had known Willie (Charles) Shealey through mutual friends. He had liked them both, but now they were gone.

I hate it. But there's nothing to be done.

Muriel doubted his good dog Sadie had survived, either. If men — most of them relatively healthy — had died, how could she have lived, especially if she was outside in low-lying land when the poisonous cloud swept through?

Assuming she had survived the initial burst, she might find water down at the creek, but where would she find food?

Muriel rubbed his hand across his gray crew-cut and straightened his shoulders. No. He doubted Sadie was alive. But there was nothing he could do for her but wait.

SHARON MCLAUGHLIN

SHARON STAYED INSIDE her house and took care of her dogs and cat. She didn't let them outside, but cleaned up after them, instead. She wasn't risking them after going through so much trouble to keep them safe.

The dogs seemed painfully embarrassed that they weren't allowed to go out, but Sharon comforted them. Clean water and cleanser would take care of the floor. It was only a minor inconvenience if it meant her babies stayed alive.

All she could do in her enforced free time was read, write, check in with friends on the telephone, and watch television coverage of the clean-up taking place on the tracks to the south of her.

The thought of a second release from the badly damaged tanker concerned her greatly. What if it tore loose in the middle of the night and her precautions in securing the house weren't enough to keep the fumes at bay? She and her pets could asphyxiate in their home.

But there was no point in worrying about it. The situation was the same. Sharon could not take her pets to safety with her, and she would not leave without them. She was at a stalemate with fate.

PAMELA HALL

SHE DROVE THROUGH AIKEN grumbling and grousing. She had rented a small house from a friend for her and her son to use and had seen the rest of her family safe with relatives. But she and Latrell had minimal clothes, no pots and pans in which to cook, and no toys to keep the boy entertained.

The Hall-Gaffney Learning Center she operated on Nivens Street was closed thanks to the evacuation. Several parents had already informed her their children would not be coming back. They were afraid to let their kids come back into Graniteville, even after the emergency was lifted.

Pamela was further angered that Latrell had required an emergency room visit in the middle of the night. Exposure to chlorine had aggravated his asthma. He was put on medication to assist his breathing, and to Pamela's shock, she was medicated as well.

The emergency room physician had insisted she needed it. She had always been a healthy person. She wasn't used to being sick.

As she grumbled to herself, Pamela glanced in the rearview mirror and saw her son and her nephew laughing and talking in the back seat. The sight of them smiling when she was so moody pulled her up short.

What are you thinking? You left everything behind, but you and your family are alive. You shouldn't be complaining. You should be thanking God for your blessings.

Pamela began to cry. She prayed aloud, "Thank you, God. Thank you, God!"

The boys looked at her, puzzled.

"Keon," Latrell said, "my mamma's having a holy."

Pamela couldn't help but laugh. "You must mean the Holy Ghost," she told him.

"That's right," Latrell said. "Yes, ma'am."

Pamela drove on, happier than she had been since she had first heard of the accident. Thanks to God's grace, she and her family were going to be all right.

SHIRLEY HARDEN

THE PHONES IN HARDEN'S OFFICE rang non-stop. Displaced residents who had left pets behind were beginning to worry, especially those forced to leave their dogs or cats at the mercy of the elements in the hot zone.

Shirley, a tall woman with her long brunette hair pulled back in a ponytail, looked around for her perpetually misplaced glasses and began to take notes. As director and shelter supervisor of Aiken County Animal Services, it was up to her to find a way to assist Graniteville's furred and feathered populations.

Shirley took her job at Animal Services at a time when women didn't often do such work. A native of Aiken, she was appointed to the 1978 Registrations and Elections Commission by Governor Dick Riley, where she stayed until 1991.

It didn't take the blunt-talking Shirley long to sicken of what she saw as crooked politics. There was too much "you scratch my back and I'll scratch yours" at the capitol. Shirley decided if there was scratching to be done, it was better done with a dog in her lap.

She applied for her original job, animal control officer, four times before she got it.

On the morning of the Graniteville disaster, Shirley had waked at 5 a.m. to a call from her boss, Aiken County Director of Public Works Alvin Bryan. He told her of the accident and asked her to go into work as soon as she could get there.

There were people trapped in Graniteville with no vehicles with which to make an escape. Animal Services employees might be called upon to transport victims in county trucks.

Shirley called in her three officers and met them at the shelter on Wire Road before dawn. By then, school buses had been deemed more practical for transporting victims to decontamination sites, and the Animal Service workers weren't needed.

They kept a weather eye on the news anyway, just the same. Aerial surveillance reports indicated animal carcasses visible on the ground. Shirley hoped that pets brought indoors might have fared better. The only way to know was to go into the evacuation zone and see.

Late on the afternoon of January 7, Shirley met with Alvin Bryan and Aiken County Administrator Clay Killigan to decide what could be done. The trick was how to enter private residences to rescue pets, without finding the county legally liable at a later date.

A call to Aiken County Attorney Robert Bell solved that problem. Residents would have to sign a waiver before Animal Services could retrieve their pets.

Shirley breathed a sigh of relief. *We have to do something. We can't just leave them there.*

Word went out through the media that Graniteville residents in the evacuation area — but outside the still simmering center of the hot zone — could go to Midland Valley High School to sign a waiver and hand over a house key.

Volunteers, including veterinarians and ordinary citizens, arrived to help with paperwork and other organizational chores. Animal lovers throughout the community brought bags of pet food and jugs of water to leave for pets that could not be safely removed from their homes.

Shirley moved through the bustle, enjoying a warm glow. It seemed strange to be happy under the circumstances, but she couldn't help it.

In the midst of tragedy, the community had not forgotten its animal friends. Some pets, at least, would be saved.

FISH KILL

FISH SWIMMING IN HORSE CREEK at the time of the accident were not quite so fortunate. As chlorine mixed with water to form hydrochloric acid, finned corpses began to pop to the surface. They floated downstream, bumping along banks and deadfalls, until they reached Langley Pond, where they spangled the water with silver and blue scales.

South Carolina Department of Health and Environmental Control investigated and discovered that more than 1800 yards of the creek had been affected, probably when chlorine vapors drifted through a storm drain behind one of the plants.

Investigators walking along the lowland closest to the spill found a desolate topography awaiting them. Trees, vines, shrubs — even cacti — were blasted and brown.

Ground-hugging junipers growing in front of mill offices were burned yellow. The little evergreen tree planted in front of the GVW fire station, always so festive with lights during the holiday season, looked as though someone had taken a blowtorch to it.

Live oaks and sweet gums along the Leitner Street Extension dropped their leaves. Crepe myrtles that had sifted pink and purple petals into the Graniteville Canal in summers past wept nothing but greasy remains of Spanish moss from thin, whitened limbs.

Still, in the midst of all this devastation, life remained. The pines, dogwoods and elms in Donnie William's yard in Rocktown were all dead. But the aged camellia shrub by his front door was speckled purple with blossoms. The glossy green leaves showed no more damage than they might have taken in an ice storm.

Over on Hester Lane, Miss Morrall's shrubs were crispy at the edges, but one of her beloved butterfly bushes promised signs of healing green. Forty of the trees in the park across the street from Sharon McLaughlin's house had succumbed to the gas, but many more remained untouched.

It seemed a random killing: one saved here, one perished there. Only the budding of the spring would prove which plants and trees in the hot zone were permanently lost, and which might hope to survive — but spring was on its way.

SHERIFF HUNT

MICHAEL HUNT HAD a lot on his mind.

Graniteville had already suffered one catastrophic release of chlorine. Manipulating the remaining cars in the wreck could easily cause another. If disaster struck twice, the evacuation might have to extend to a three-mile radius, displacing three times as many people.

Sheriff Hunt spent the second day of the emergency in briefings with specialists from all over the country, determining how best to deal with a second evacuation, if it came.

The initial news was not promising. Aiken Regional Medical Centers, USC Aiken and numerous nursing homes — not to mention businesses, residences and hotels already stuffed with the first round of evacuees — were all within the second potential danger zone.

The Sheriff asked Aiken County Emergency Preparedness to put the National Guard on stand-by in case they were needed. It would be difficult, if not impossible, to move so many people without help.

But by 3 p.m., the Sheriff and the others in unified command could breathe a little easier. Models showed that a second release would follow approximately the same boundaries as the first. The one-mile radius evacuation was sufficient for now.

This news gave the Sheriff the room he needed to concentrate on his next priority: protecting Graniteville from would-be thieves and vandals.

The roadblocks and dusk to dawn curfew remained in effect. Four individuals had violated the curfew the night before and were arrested within the evacuation zone. Two were arrested for alcohol and marijuana offenses. Two others were wanted on outstanding warrants.

The Sheriff wanted a strong message sent: Theft in Graniteville would not be tolerated while its residents were displaced. He and his men patrolled the village in a 24-hour operation for the next 14 days to ensure just that.

At the end of it, he would be proud to report that not a single break-in took place within the boundaries of the evacuation zone while the curfew was in effect.

NORFOLK SOUTHERN

AS DUSK FELL, Norfolk Southern contractors continued to work containing and cleaning up the spill and the accompanying train wreckage. They removed debris that circled the cracked tanker so they could patch the breach without hindrance.

Forty tons of crushed lime was scattered at ground zero to neutralize chlorine on the soil. Empty tankers were set into place so the liquid chlorine in the two remaining cars could be transferred and removed.

Work was again suspended at dawn so the search for Willie Tyler could continue. Rescuers would not stop looking until they found him.

DAY 3

JANUARY 8, 2005

ED SCHULER

FRIDAY PASSED IN A BLUR. On Saturday, Ed prepared to join a team of 13 to again search the Woodhead Division for Willie Tyler, the only Avondale employee still missing.

Ed knew — as all the responders did — there was little hope of finding Mr. Tyler alive. But Ed felt he owed it to the man's family to try. He couldn't imagine what they must be going through as they waited for word.

The team asked for a map of Woodhead, but none was immediately available. There was one, however, rolled up in a piece of plastic pipe at the plant entrance. That would have to do.

Ed and his team split up, six entering the plant and seven waiting outside as backup. They were forced to wear respirators in case there were pockets of chlorine still lurking inside.

The six-member team split yet again, half circling the plant clockwise and half circling windershins. The interior of the low-slung metal building was dank and dark.

Its trademark colony of harmless daddy longlegs, which had once scurried up the walls on hair-thin legs, was gone. The birds that had nested in the rafters were silent. Nothing but Ed and his teammates moved within.

The team had thought they would find Mr. Tyler in the paint shop where he worked, but he was not there. They continued to search, one square at a time, but within 45 minutes they were running out of air and were forced to exit. They searched outside, but found nothing but twisted shrubs and blasted grass.

A second round of teams went in, this time conducting an arm-length search, in which rescuers walked side by side but one arm's length apart. They were preparing to exit for the second time when a shadow on the floor coalesced into the shape of a man.

Willie Tyler was found 20 yards within the front entrance of the plant, lying beneath a chunk of heavy equipment that had shielded him from view. The team must have passed him at least twice without noticing him.

Ed let out a breath of relief. The news was bad. It was terrible. But at least the Tyler family would know what had happened, at last.

BOB DOWNING

BOB AND HIS FAMILY had good news. Evacuated streets were being re-occupied, one by one, as air quality within the village improved. Trollyline Road and Laurel Drive were among the first to re-open, so Bob, his wife, and their four dogs went home.

The house appeared no different. The trees and plants in the garden remained unscorched. But there was still a faint odor of bleach in the air.

Bob's dogs paid no attention. They romped in the yard, glad to be out on grass again. They had been confined in a basement for three days, let out only for leashed walks around a yard not their own.

They, like Bob and his wife, were glad to be home.

MARK BROOME

AFTER THREE DAYS in the hospital, Mark Broome came home. He went straight to his room and closed the door. He wanted to sleep.

As the days passed, David Horne watched his stepson struggle to recover. Mark's health was shaky, but it was his nerves that were worrisome. He no longer liked to drive at night. If there was fog on the road, he flatly refused to leave home.

He was quiet and introspective, and having panic attacks, when he had always been self-sufficient and well grounded before.

David couldn't blame him for his feelings. Mark had been friends with John Laird. They had grown up together. John had died in the brush behind the Woodhead Division.

Mark, against all odds, had survived. That in itself was a lot for Mark to think about.

But there was more. At 18, the young man still had his life ahead of him. Now that he was no longer working in the mill, he had no idea what he was going to do with it. Nothing much appealed to him, but he would have to do something.

Only time and healing would help him find his way.

NORFOLK SOUTHERN

NORFOLK SOUTHERN HAD WORRIES besides the clean-up taking place in Graniteville. In nearby Aiken, lines snaked in all directions from the First Presbyterian Church as villagers affected by the crisis queued up to request financial assistance.

People needed help, but there were those who refused to take it once they noticed the language on the backs of the reimbursement checks: "Endorsement of this check constitutes a full, final and complete release of all claims growing out of an accident occurring at Graniteville on 1-6-2005."

Whether it was meant that way or not, to people who already in a perilous state, the phrasing sounded an awful lot like: "We'll pay your hotel bill, but after this you're on your own."

Responding to indignant inquiries, Norfolk Southern rushed to remove the offending language from subsequent checks and released a statement within a week to assure villagers that accepting assistance now would not "preclude submission of personal injury claims, claims for subsequently incurred incidental expenses, and unforeseen property damage in the future."

Most doubters were appeased, especially after a circuit court judge ruled that the language did not, in fact, constitute a release. But there were those who, now made suspicious, refused to sign anything Norfolk Southern might hand them.

Churches and civic organizations began to gather cash donations, just in case suspicion or stubbornness prevented anyone from getting help when they needed it most. They were there to assist.

And then, there was the tradition of neighbor helping neighbor that still flourishes in Horse Creek Valley.

Horse Creek Valley is perhaps not unique in the United States, but it is certainly unusual. It is comprised of a series of small villages and towns, beginning with Stieffeltown and ending with Clearwater, that are aligned like pearls on a string between the clasps of the larger cities of Aiken and North Augusta.

In between are Warrenville, Graniteville, Langley, Burnettown and Bath, among others. Each village is in turn divided into neighborhoods with names that are apt to be recognized only if one lives in the Valley.

Good neighbors that they are, the villagers of Horse Creek Valley still tend to be a bit territorial. Old timers remember feuds between high schools, feuds between families, feuds between one neighborhood and another. Some of those hard feelings still simmer beneath the surface.

But one hard and fast rule that holds all villagers together is they are all a part of Horse Creek Valley. If trouble comes, they work together.

With that understanding, neighbors who might have barely acknowledged each other before the disaster now offered food, shelter, a "loan" of a few bucks that they did not expect repaid.

They offered each other rides to the Norfolk Southern assistance center, to the hospital, to the store. They traded babysitting duties so parents with small children in the grip of cabin fever wouldn't break down once and for all.

As sure as death and taxes, trouble would visit Horse Creek Valley again some day. When that happened, these "favors" that were not favors would not be forgotten.

DAYS 4&5

JANUARY 8 & 9, 2005

JOHN HENRY LAIRD JR.

ON SUNDAY, JANUARY 9, John Henry Laird Jr. was laid to rest.

A lead machine operator with the Avondale Mills for five years, Mr. Laird, 24, was a man who liked to work with his hands. He enjoyed tinkering on cars with his father. He loved to watch racing. But he went to church on Sundays before indulging in his love of NASCAR.

He was eulogized in his home church of Breezy Hill Baptist and buried in the Warrenville Cemetery. He was survived by his parents and step-parents, siblings and grand-parents.

CLEAN UP

AS FAMILY AND FRIENDS prayed for Mr. Laird, the clean up continued near the woods where he had perished.

With the ground around the fractured tanker now cleared of debris, Norfolk Southern contractors tackled the tricky job of securing the leaking tank. Working slowly and carefully, they turned the tanker 90 degrees so they could reach the tear.

Thirty tons of liquid chlorine scrimmed with ice rested in the curve beneath the split in the tanker's side, slowly sending tendrils of gas into the air. Vapors and liquid would be removed once the slit was sealed.

The metal sides of the tank were crumpled and warped — too warped, workers soon learned, to hold the steel patch they had cobbled to seal the breach. A temporary polyethylene patch was a snug fit, but it would have to be replaced with something stronger before the chlorine was off-loaded.

Off-loading required a vacuum process. The patch had to be sturdy enough to withstand the pressure.

The tanker containing sodium hydroxide was not as difficult to manage. It was moved a short distance from the crash site without incident. Meanwhile, workers laid more than a hundred feet of temporary track to move empty tank cars into place.

GOOD NEW AND BAD NEWS

IN SPITE OF THE CONTINUING LEAK from the broken tanker, Horse Creek was recovering.

Environmental sampling of the creek and Langley Pond found hundreds of dead fish, but chlorine in the creek had returned to pre-incident levels. Chlorine levels in the pond were slightly higher than in the creek, but were no longer present in dangerous concentrations.

Graniteville residents were working on recovery, too. They attended meetings at USC Aiken hosted by the Aiken/Barnwell Mental Health Center and the International Critical Incident Stress Foundation to learn about what was happening in their village and to receive crisis counseling.

Most were still out of their homes, traveling to Clearwater on the far side of Horse Creek Valley for such simple tasks as shopping or picking up their mail.

But they had hope. The evacuation and curfew was still in effect, but the United States Department of Health and Environmental Control had released guidelines on how to return home safely. That meant — they hoped — that they wouldn't be out of Graniteville much longer. Surely they would go home soon.

STEVEN WAYNE BAGBY SR.

HIS FAMILY WAS SAFE at home in Augusta, Ga., but that must have been a bitter comfort.

Mr. Bagby was not with them. One of the victims of the disaster, the 38-year-old hunter and fisherman had worked as a forklift operator at Avondale Mills. His family buried him on Monday, January 10.

Mr. Bagby was survived by a fiance, a father, a handful of siblings, and Steven Wayne Bagby Jr., an infant son who was only 10 days old on the day of his father's death.

SHERIFF HUNT

HE WAS A VERY ANGRY MAN.

The disaster was barely five days old, and already reports were coming in of people attempting to alter their driver's licenses to reflect a Graniteville address.

Proving a Graniteville residence would permit them to apply for financial assistance from Norfolk Southern. They would benefit from other people's pain.

Sheriff Hunt did not quite share in the general consensus of genuine Graniteville residents: Those attempting to perpetuate the fraud should fry.

He did regret that under the South Carolina Code of Laws (56-1-510-Unlawful Use of a License; Fraudulent

Application), those caught trying to use false documentation for personal gain could be charged with nothing but a misdemeanor, punishable by a fine of up to $200 or thirty days in jail.

They deserved, the Sheriff thought, a great deal more than that.

DAY 6

JANUARY 11, 2005

CLEAN UP

ON THE MORNING OF TUESDAY, JANUARY 11, the cracked tanker finally got its permanent steel patch. Workers used a backhoe to pound the steel into a shape that would match the twisted tanker — an innovative tactic, but an effective one.

Holes drilled into the patch were matched with holes drilled into the tanker. Before lag bolts were installed and tightened, black putty was smeared between the two metal pieces to assure an airtight seal.

Once the patch was securely in place, workers applied hot air blowers similar to gigantic hair dryers to the outside ends of the tank to warm the chlorine inside. As the tank heated, the liquid chlorine vaporized, allowing it to be drawn off with hoses.

This was done only with the damaged tanker. The two other tankers, whose loads remained uncompromised, had their contents directly transferred into other tank cars.

While contractors worked at unloading the tankers, other agencies were busy throughout the village. The EPA monitored the air quality in the Gregg Plant to determine when the building might be reoccupied. DHEC and the Department of Natural Resources revisited Langley Pond to determine if the fish kill was large enough to warrant the disposal of carcasses.

They found a "relatively small" kill of less than 1,000 fish — but 1,000 decomposing fish smelled like a twice that amount. Norfolk Southern agreed to arrange for the disposal, much to the relief of residents living near the pond.

The Aiken County Sheriff's Department was busy,

too. More than 60 people had attempted to alter their driver's licenses in order to request financial assistance from Norfolk Southern. Deputies were only too happy to arrest them when they were caught.

Volunteers with the GVW Fire Department still struggled with the fire at the Stevens Steam Plant, which stubbornly refused to stay out. They installed water monitors that sent a constant flow of water over the smoldering coal chutes. The fire finally relented, but not for another five days.

Just as the clean up seemed to be progressing smoothly, reports came of natural gas leaks on Main Street. One worker reported natural gas hissing from a manhole cover. Corrosion had attacked meters and pipes.

Chief Napier, exhausted after days of work on little or no sleep, heard of the newest twist in the crisis from the secondary staging area at Honda Cars of Aiken. He slumped to the floor and sat for a while, despairing.

How much more can we take? Haven't we had enough?

Shirley Harden at Aiken County Animal Services was hearing bad news, too. Six of the pets rescued from the edges of the hot zone had sickened and died.

She and local veterinarians warned pet owners to watch their animals carefully for signs of illness so they could seek immediate treatment. It was possible some of the animals had ingested chlorine through contaminated food or water.

The only good news, it seemed, was for Aiken County parents. Children had returned to school after the extended winter holidays, only to be yanked out again three days later when the disaster struck.

Now all but Leavelle McCampbell Middle School, Byrd Elementary and Freedman Alternative School were preparing to reopen. Parents and children alike breathed a sigh of relief. Time off was fun, but too much of it was wearing. It would be nice to get back to normal again.

BEN COCHRAN

HE HAD LITTLE RECOLLECTION of the accident. It was hard for him to distinguish between what co-workers had told him and his own scattered memories. But he did remember the onset of his asthma attack.

A resin range, which heats and stretches cloth, had blown a torque motor. Ben was repairing it when his boss sent him to the supply room for parts.

Looking over the shelves, searching for the bits and pieces he needed, Ben took a breath that staggered him. He grabbed for the inhaler in his pocket, but it was too late. He was already in trouble. He stumbled from the room and fell.

That was the last clear memory Ben could claim from the incident. He knew a co-worker helped him outside. He knew Mike Lambert and Curtis found him and dragged him to the lab, where Curtis bathed him in water and ice in a futile attempt to revive him.

He vaguely remembered muttering to Mike, “I’m not going to make it,” and Mike responding, “Yes. Yes, you are.”

No one believed it, though. Ben’s friends thought he was going to die.

Thirty minutes passed, and the ambulance Ben's co-workers had summoned didn't come. Big Mike, a boss in the plant, took matters into his own hands and dragged Ben outside in an attempt to reach a truck he could use to get him to the hospital. When they reached a stairway, Big Mike picked Ben up and carried him up the flight as though he were a child.

Once beside the truck, Big Mike put Ben down and sat on the ground beside him, panting. They waited a few more minutes for an ambulance, but when none came, he gave up and loaded Ben into the cab.

"He must have been flying," Ben recalled, "because someone told my father later that I'd been transported by helicopter. That's how fast Big Mike was driving. I didn't get to the hospital by helicopter. I got there on a rice rocket."

Big Mike got Ben to safety before collapsing in a hospital hallway. He was admitted to the hospital himself while Ben was taken to intensive care.

Ben stayed deep in an anesthetic fog for four days. He woke with a sore chest, but a heart that hurt even more.

His first words were, "Where's my baby?"

Ben knew he had been in a terrible accident. He was concerned about his daughter, who was worried sick about him.

Dana came in to see him for the first time since the disaster.

She cried.

FRED (RUSTY) RUSHTON III

DANA'S WERE NOT THE ONLY tears flowing that day. Friends and family of Rusty Rushton crowded the Langley Community Center to honor his memory. So many came that the chairs and aisles overflowed and latecomers were obliged to stand outside, clustered around the opened doors.

Mr. Rushton, 41, was a blond, stocky man with an outgoing personality and a generous heart that had survived earlier hardships that might have left him bitter. A lifelong resident of Aiken County, he had graduated from Midland Valley High School.

He was a hard worker and a devoted father, but he was also a free spirit. He was enamored of his bright red Honda Shadow Saber 1100, which he had playfully christened "Reba." He loved music, dancing and the beach.

Not many who came to honor him were surprised when the music of his service was comprised largely of "Margaritaville" and other of Jimmy Buffet's greatest hits.

Kim, the woman he considered his lifelong partner, saw to it that he was outfitted in his favorite jeans, black oxford shirt and leather jacket. A Jimmy Buffet pin inscribed "Changes in Latitudes, Changes in Attitudes" was pinned to his chest. Kim wore its twin.

Later, Kim and other members of Rusty's family did what he would have wanted. They scattered a handful of his ashes at the beach, so he would be forever free.

CHRISTOPHER SEELING

THE ENGINEER OF TRAIN 192 was also laid to rest on January 11.

He has always wanted to be an engineer, from the time he was a little boy growing up in Kansas. He loved to hunt and fish, but trains were his first passion. After attending community college, he joined Norfolk Southern, beginning as a conductor and working his way up to the job he was born to have.

Mr. Seeling, 28, was survived by his parents, stepparents, four sisters, two brothers and his grandfathers.

DAY 7

JANUARY 12, 2005

LAMAR LEDFORD

LAMAR SPENT SIX DAYS recuperating at Aiken Regional Medical Centers. While there, he was reunited with his friend Patrick. He had made it out of the plant, but had spent three days at University Hospital in Augusta after driving through the worst of the cloud.

Lamar checked out of ARMC on Wednesday, January 12, with a brace on his foot — but no oxygen canister, for which he thanked God. He returned to the family farm where his ancestors had once grown corn, melons and cotton.

He stayed with his grandmother, Clara Roland. Lamar's mother's house suffered from a mild mold problem, common in the south — a problem which had never bothered Lamar before, but which now left him coughing.

In the days following the accident, coughing wasn't all of Lamar's problems. He was haunted by the idea that if he had died, he would have forced his mother to witness his death. He woke screaming in the night, shaking from nightmares he couldn't remember.

He knew he needed professional counseling, but he wasn't up for it yet.

"I need to back away from it a little first," he told his family. "I thought I was going to die in there."

"People ask how I got out," he added slowly, meditatively. "It wasn't strength or fate or faith. It was just fear. I didn't want to die on the floor of a textile mill."

SHARON MCLAUGHLIN

SHE HAD FINALLY let her dogs venture outside on Sunday, after noticing a squirrel in the yard. The furry little rodent was the first sign of life she had seen since the accident. The dogs didn't stay out long, but they seemed jubilant to see the sun again.

Sharon understood how they felt. She was tired of being inside, too.

Wednesday morning, she let them out again while she tended to some necessary housework. All of a sudden, Bert went wild. He was barking and jumping and baying all at once.

Sharon looked out and saw a man pouring half a bag of dog food over her fence.

"Oh, no!" she cried, scaring the Animal Services officer half out of his wits.

Oh, yes! Bert seemed to say, gobbling free food as fast as he could swallow.

It was too late to stop him. Sharon let him eat. She went out to speak to the officers, a man and woman team.

"We thought we had overlooked some dogs," the officer she had startled said. "We're feeding the ones we find. But we didn't expect to see anyone here."

"I've been here all along," Sharon said. "But I need some groceries. I'm almost out."

The officers offered to take her out of the evacuation zone so she could buy food, but she was worried she wouldn't be allowed back in again. A phone call to the police confirmed that.

If she left, Sharon would not be allowed to return, even

though the barricade surrounding the evacuation zone had been shortened to a mere two houses away from her front door.

"How would it be if I called a friend to shop for me and have her bring the food to the barricade?" Sharon asked. "Can I come get it and have it handed to me over the bar?"

"If you stay on the sidewalk," the officer said.

Sharon snorted. *What do they think? I'm going to load it in a wheelbarrow and trundle it down the middle of the street?*

But she didn't say anything. She knew everyone working the disaster must be on the edge of exhaustion by now. Tempers were bound to be short.

She thanked the officer for his time and hung up so she could call a friend to shop for her.

CHIEF NAPIER

NAPIER AND HIS MEN finally got to inspect their Main Street firehouse on the seventh day following the disaster. HAZMATers who had toured the place had already warned them of what they would find. But Chief Napier could hardly believe his eyes.

Metal doorknobs and hinges were green. The station's stainless steel ice machine was corroded a rusty brown. Fire truck grills and the chrome on the station's first response ambulance dripped green icicles, as though they had rested on the ocean floor for the past hundred years.

The wiring inside the vehicles was eaten away. Two engines, the ambulance and a service truck, would have to be totaled and hauled away.

Totaling the firehouse itself was out of the question. The department didn't carry enough insurance to afford it. The metal house, faded brown from its original red, would have to be scrubbed and rewired. Its fixtures would have to be replaced. But it would go back into use.

In the meantime, the department had a temporary home on Ascauga Lake Road, when Norfolk Southern rented the old Community Services building and permitted the fire department to set up shop in the back.

We're crippled, the Chief thought, *but we're not out.*

The department still had Stations Two and Three on Ascauga Lake Road, both equipped with undamaged trucks and gear. The Chief ordered a fire truck moved from Station Two to temporary headquarters. Meanwhile, the Belvedere Volunteer Fire Department loaned GVW a pumper.

We'll just have to go on from here.

AVONDALE MILLS

WORKERS AT THE AVONDALE FACILITIES were facing much the same situation, though perhaps not quite so dire. The chlorine had damaged machinery and stock, but not as badly as originally feared.

The computers in the Information Services Building close to the crash were beyond salvage, their circuit boards chewed by chlorine. But the information they had once contained was backed up elsewhere.

Inside the plants themselves, machinery had fared better, although they were crusted with salts left behind when chlorine reacted with their metals. They would have to be cleaned, re-oiled and re-greased. Chlorine reacted with lubricants, too.

Clean up crews set up camp outside the Woodhead Division. They would not leave for weeks to come.

CLEAN UP

AFTER THE SECOND TANKER of chlorine was offloaded during the night of January 11, workers began working on the third and final car. This would take an additional 16 to 24 hours.

Twenty-six monitoring units placed by the EPA, the U.S. Coast Guard and CTEH continued to sample the air, guarding against the hazard of a second release.

Kaolin — the white powder that had so alarmed Ed Schuler when it coated his suit after his fall down the railroad embankment — and diesel fuel was also part of the clean up.

Fortunately, the tanker loaded with sodium hydroxide had not spilled.

Gradually, street by street, Graniteville residents began to return to the edges of their village. They showed proof of residence at traffic control points and went home to scrub walls and floors, discard open packages of food, and open windows to give their houses a good airing.

The mills were reviving, too. Sharon McLaughlin woke one night to a heavy rushing sound. She got out of bed, sleepily making her way to the porch, assuming a water pipe must have burst.

As she fully wakened, she realized what she was hearing. The rush was the sound of a mill clearing its throat. Swint, Townsend and Horse Creek Divisions of Avondale Mills were resuming partial operations.

Graniteville was slowly beginning to stir. However, residents of the hot zone still remained in exile.

JOANNE LEOPARD

THE NOISE FROM THE CLEAN UP was wearing on Joanne's nerves. The clank and rattle and rumble of machinery never stopped. An older woman with children and grandchildren, she fervently wished for a night of unbroken sleep.

She woke often in the night, her heart pounding and her mouth dry. Her Maltese pup comforted her, put she, too, was upset by the noise. Candy stayed close, ears perked at the racket.

On the morning of January 12, four officers knocked on Joanne's door. Her landlord had wondered why she was not among the evacuees and had sent the law to check on her.

Until that moment, officers had no reason to suspect there was anyone living on Swint Street. Snugged deep into a side cut of woods, Joanne's mobile home was hard to find.

Joanne felt sorry for the officers. They looked haggard and worn, as though they hadn't slept in days. She assured them she was fine. Even though she was inside the radius of the mandatory evacuation zone, they did not insist that she leave.

When they left her, Joanne went back inside her home and closed the door. She hoped life would return to normal by the weekend.

JOSEPH STONE

LIFE MUST HAVE SEEMED anything but normal to the family of Joseph Stone. The 22-year-old truck driver with the dark hair, green eyes and open smile had left his previous job as a welder because the fumes irritated his asthma.

He had worked for J.W. Service and Express out of Deauville, Quebec, for less than four months when he drove into Graniteville to make a delivery at the Avondale Mills.

Mr. Stone arrived at the end of a shift change. He called his girlfriend back home in Sherbrooke, Quebec, to let her know he had opted to sleep in his cab that night so he could unload his cargo in the morning.

He was overcome by chlorine poisoning before dawn.

Mr. Stone's funeral was held January 12 at Standstead Wesleyan United Church in Quebec. His co-workers sent a funeral arrangement in the shape of his truck.

His family wrote to South Carolina newspapers, both in Aiken and Columbia, to thank the community for their kindness to their son, a child lost far from home.

WILLIE CHARLES SHEALEY

THE SAME DAY MR. STONE'S FAMILY was mourning their son, the family of Willie Charles Shealey was mourning his death.

A lifelong resident of Aiken County, Mr. Shealey was a graduate of Leavelle McCampbell, when the school was still a high school. He loved horses and was a member of the New Ellenton Riding Club.

A member of the National Guard 122nd Engineer Company in Graniteville, he was also a third shift supervisor in the Avondale Mills.

Mr. Shealey was known as a steady and responsible man. His dedication to his job may have cost him his life. When he learned of the chlorine spill, he didn't run, but stopped to turn off machinery and help others out of the Woodhead Division.

He and John Henry Laird, among the last to leave, had tried to help each other. They were found arm in arm in the woods behind the plant, where they had attempted to outrun the cloud.

Mr. Shealey was survived by his wife of more than 20 years, three sons, and a number of siblings.

His co-workers called him a hero.

DAY 8&9

JANUARY 13 & 14, 2005

CLEAN UP

THE TANKERS WERE EMPTY at last. They were washed inside and out, then loaded onto flat cars and moved away from the derailment site. Repairs on the mangled track could now begin.

Graniteville continued to gasp its way back to life. Main Street re-opened between S.C. Highway 421 and U.S. Highway 1, allowing a handful of residents to return home. However, most downtown businesses were still in what was considered the hot zone.

Chlorine levels were dropping, but scares were still possible. A reading of .7 parts per million spiked at the crash site, but returned to zero within seconds.

A United States Environmental Protection Agency emergency response team veterinarian arrived to coordinate with Animal Services for the removal of animal carcasses near the crash site.

The carcasses were themselves contaminated. Graniteville residents were warned not to touch any dead creatures they might find, but to report them, instead.

SHIRLEY HARDEN

AIKEN COUNTY ANIMAL SERVICES worked 94 hours the week following the disaster, assisted by representatives from the Aiken Department of Public Safety, Lexington County Animal Control and Clemson University.

They went from house to house, luring frightened cats

from beneath beds and retrieving dogs from bathrooms, bedrooms and hallways.

In all, 314 dogs and cats, 20 birds, two hamsters, a ferret and a rabbit went into carriers that were loaded onto the back of trucks for transport to Midland Valley High School, where their owners were waiting to claim them.

Twenty-seven animals were discovered dead in their yards or homes. Shirley called their owners to break the news. She comforted them as they cried, and wept herself in private.

While they pursued their rescue mission, officers sometimes paused long enough to fulfill a special request residents had made of them.

One homeowner asked that someone check to see if her coffee pot was still burning on her kitchen counter. Another asked for food and water for what appeared to be an oversized wharf rat, but which was, nevertheless, someone's cherished pet.

In the midst of the rescue effort, an enormous bouquet of flowers arrived at Shirley's office. The card read "From a Grateful Citizen."

Shirley Harden broke down in tears.

"I'm just grateful we were able to do something for people," she said later. "It was a terrible disaster. But those were good days for us."

JOANNE LEOPARD

SHE STOOD IN HER YARD, more unnerved than she had been since the morning of the wreck. A strong chemical odor permeated the air.

Joanne opened the doors on her aging car and started scrubbing out the interior, which stank of bleach. The exterior was a lost cause. Peeling paint marred the wheel wells and side panels. The chrome of the grill was spotted black and brown.

Joanne did the best she could, but saw little progress. Just as she was finishing up, a female officer from the Beaufort County Sheriff's Office arrived with food and drinks.

She told Joanne that one of the tankers was still leaking traces of chlorine. Graniteville residents in other parts of the evacuation zone were going home, but Joanne should think of leaving.

"It's best to leave," she said. "I'll show you where to go."

Exhausted and lonely after a week on her own, Joanne agreed. She put Candy in the car and followed the officer to the command center.

But her troubles were not yet over. She had only recently moved to Swint Street, and while she had paperwork to prove it, her address was not yet reflected on her driver's license.

Convincing officials that yes, there was a street next to Powell, and yes, Joanne lived on it, took some doing. The officer that had led her to the command center finally intervened. Joanne blessed her for it. She was too tired to argue anymore.

That night she slept away from noise since the first morning of the disaster. She still felt nervous and shaky. But at least she was safe.

ALLEN FRAZIER

ON THURSDAY, JANUARY 13, Allen Frazier, 58, of Ridge Spring, was quietly laid to rest at Bethlehem Baptist Church in Edgefield.

The Avondale employee, reported to be an avid fisherman, was survived by his wife, three children, five grandchildren, and several siblings.

WILLIE LEE TYLER

THE GENTLE MAN that Liz Pulver remembered for his good nature and melodious voice was eulogized the same day.

Willie Lee Tyler, 57, was a deacon of the Sardis Baptist Church in Salley. He used the gift of music he believed his Lord had given him to found Deacon Willie Tyler and the Gospel Jewels.

He had also worked with The Fantastic Melodairs. He was proud of a gospel song he had composed called "The Same Train."

Deacon Tyler was also a family man, devoted to his wife. A paint mixer in the Woodhead Division, he had changed his shift so he could give her more attentive care.

He was survived by his wife, two daughters, five grandchildren, and his sisters and brothers.

DAY 10

JANUARY 15, 2005

MIKE LAMBERT

MIKE WAS IN THE INTENSIVE CARE UNIT of University Hospital for six days. He didn't wake until the fourth. He had broken recollections of his girlfriend, Kay, looking after him, and of his family and friends gathered around him.

He remembered his pastor, the Rev. Buster Youngblood of Saluda River Bible Hour, praying for him. He remembered whispering, "I might not make it, Reverend, but that's all right."

He remembered feeling at peace.

On the Saturday, January 15, Mike left the hospital with an oxygen canister trailing behind him. He carried it with him for three weeks. It was a dreadful inconvenience, but, it beat not breathing.

His voice was hoarse. His eyes were red. His breath was a sharp whistle in his throat. But he was alive.

When he was able to get around without help, Mike found a nickel on the dash of his truck. The coin looked as though someone had dipped it in acid. He left it where it lay. He would get another truck. His was too contaminated to keep.

In the weeks following the disaster, Mike thought often of his friends who didn't survive. He had known Tony DeLoach well. He grieved for him, especially.

But Mike held no anger for Norfolk Southern, nor for the men accused of failing to trip the switch that led to the accident.

"Why should I be angry?" Mike asked. "I used to be a heavy drinker, before I sobered up. There was many a night I climbed into my truck so drunk I couldn't see, and somehow

I made it home. I could have wiped out a school bus full of kids and I wouldn't have known it.

"We have all made mistakes in our lives that could have turned out bad. Those men who made this mistake are no different. They should be lifted up in prayer. No matter what they did or didn't do, they are still children of God."

CLEAN UP

THE AIKEN COUNTY SCHOOL DISTRICT went to extraordinary lengths to ensure that parents felt safe allowing their children to return to school.

Byrd Elementary and Leavelle McCampbell were set to open on Tuesday, following the Martin Luther King Jr. holiday. Before then, every surface in the two schools was scrubbed clean. Air quality was tested and proven safe.

Parents were reassured the Aiken County School District had checked electrical, plumbing, computer and alarm systems and had found them all in order.

In the cafeterias, all food, except unopened canned goods, was discarded and replaced. Heating and air filters were replaced and fresh air cycled through the buildings several times. Open houses were scheduled for Martin Luther King Jr. Day, so parents could visit the schools and see for themselves that all was well.

Sheriff Hunt offered reassurances of his own.

"You can call it the Mike Junior Test," he said. "I've only got the one boy, and if it's not safe, he won't be there."

Homeowners needed reassurances of their own. The Center for Toxicology and Environmental Health and the

U.S. Environmental Protection Agency conducted nearly 500 home inspections as more people returned to the village.

All results were negative.

A strip of Rocktown still remained uninhabitable, however. Donnie Williams was still in his hotel room, surrounded by his neighbors. He was told his house was likely damaged, but that Norfolk Southern would take care of the repairs.

Donnie didn't worry about it. The house, dear as it was to him, was replaceable. He was alive. That was what counted.

Meanwhile, on the tracks only a few hundred feet from Donnie's back door, 13 rail cars loaded with scrap metal, paper and other debris from the crash waited to leave the area.

Norfolk Southern re-railed three locomotives toppled in the derailment. The chlorine transfer continued from the damaged rail car, but it was nearing completion, as were track repairs and soil removal from the tainted ground.

Now that the town was reviving, Norfolk Southern prepared to move its local assistance center to the former Community Services building on Ascauga Lake Road, where they could serve residents more handily. More than 3,000 people had already sought assistance.

Some would still need help as they repaired their home, continued to seek medical treatment, or waited to return to their jobs in businesses that remained closed.

TONY DELOACH

ON THE AFTERNOON OF JANUARY 15, Graniteville said goodbye to the Shrimp Man.

Tony DeLoach, a man who had lost much of his eyesight in Vietnam, suffered from emphysema and pain in his knees that would have required knee replacement surgery had he lived.

He earned his nickname from the fresh shrimp he sold on Main Street. Passerby would honk their horns at him. Mr. DeLoach would wave back.

His family and friends remembered that he had never lost his sense of patriotism and was proud to be a Marine. He was also a former employee of the Avondale Mills.

Mr. DeLoach, 56, was buried with military honors in the Graniteville Cemetery. He was survived by his mother, three sons, a daughter, his brother and sister, and eight grandchildren.

DAY 11

JANUARY 16, 2005

CLEAN UP

NORFOLK SOUTHERN CONTRACTORS began to finish up the last details of the clean up at the derailment site. The three re-railed locomotives were moved. Rail cars carrying freight and debris departed that Sunday night.

Contaminated soil was removed from the site and fresh soil applied. The Canal Street park, which had taken a hard blow from the chlorine, was beautified with rye and fescue seeds applied to the ground. The seeds sprouted within days — a hopeful sight amidst patches that remained brown.

Meanwhile, air and surface sampling was completed at the Aiken County Magistrate Office and the bank complex in Masonic Shopping Center. No chlorine was detected.

First Baptist Church was also given the all clear, but did not escape undamaged. Its organ and pianos would have to be repaired or replaced. Chlorine, it seemed, played hell on piano strings.

BEN COCHRAN & REGINA READY

LIKE MANY OF THE PEOPLE affected by the disaster, Ben Cochran and Regina Ready found that their altered lives chafed at them once they returned home.

Ben and his daughter loved to ride go-carts together. The entire family were avid NASCAR fans and followed the races. Everyone in the family worked hard. Now their hours circled around Ben's doctor's appointments and his four-times-a-day breathing treatments.

"All they can tell us is 'I don't know' and 'long term

implications may be...'" Regina said. "We wait to see how the doctors say our lives are going to be, but they can't tell us anything definitive. It's so frustrating!"

And, she thought, *frightening.*

Ben silently agreed. Always a quiet man, he had become quieter still. He stayed close to home, where he wouldn't have to deal with people unexpectedly.

His emotions were still uncomfortably close to the surface; he didn't like anyone to see him if his control wavered. So Ben stayed inside with his family and spoiled his little Pomeranian even more than usual.

The keys that had been in his pocket the day of the disaster shed green and rust-colored particles into the plastic bag that held them. They reminded him just how close he had come to dying.

Knowing it was bad enough — tossing the keys away wouldn't take the memory with them. But Ben had been good friends with Rusty Rushton and Allen Frazier. He had seen Rusty the week before in a local motorcycle shop. He thought of Allen as a nice fellow, worthy of friendship and respect.

Ben had lived when they had not.

He grieved for them both.

DAY 12

JANUARY 17, 2005

MURIEL COOK

HE DIDN'T GO HOME for nine days. He arrived just in time for an ice storm that froze the weekend solid, ending the mild weather for the next few weeks.

He dreaded turning up Hester Lane. He didn't want to see what he knew he would find.

But when the tarmac turned to the earth of Muriel's yard, there was Sadie, running circles around his truck and leaping for joy. She was none the worse for wear. She hadn't even lost any weight.

Clean-up crews and HAZMAT teams had discovered a seriously possessive dog guarding the hardware store and mobile home at the end of Hester Lane. They had bribed her back to her natural sweetness with a steady diet of hamburgers and leftover french fries.

Miss Morrall didn't come home for another five days. She was grieving for her place. Muriel worried that her health would fail her.

Once she was back with her family and her garden, she improved. Most of her outdoor plants were dead. Spring would mean replanting. But that, at least, gave her something to anticipate.

Muriel waited until the Tuesday after he got home to walk down to the creek.

The lush greenery that had always thrived in the harshest of southern winters was brittle and brown. There was no sign of fish. Those that had succumbed to the fish kill following the accident had already floated down the creek to Langley Pond.

But the water rushed by over the white sand, just as it always had.

The fish would come back. They always had.

In the days following his return, Muriel was glad to have life back to normal. The friends that traditionally gathered at his hardware store on Sunday mornings to gossip and tell tall tales were back.

Sadie lounged in the yard, tongue lolling over her smile, and greeted people as they came in. Miss Morrall was thinking about her spring garden. Life was almost as it was.

Almost.

"If there's one thing I've noticed," Muriel observed to his friends, "it's that the trains have slowed way down. I'm glad of that. It's less hazardous. They might have a chance to correct a mistake. They were going way too fast, before."

SKIP TO

DAYS 14&15

JANUARY 19 & 20, 2005

GRANITEVILLE'S HEART BEGAN to beat again. Businesses along Main Street received permission to open. Some, such as Dale's convenience store, would have to be rewired. The wiring had been eaten by chlorine.

Restaurants, such as Bush's Seafood and Graniteville's landmark, Blue Top — famous for its burgers and blue plate specials — would have to scrub down everything, and in some cases, replace their stock.

But at least business could begin to return to normal. Signs went up in front of buildings: Welcome Home, Graniteville. The flag in front of the old GVW firehouse flew at half-staff.

Seventy-five residents along Canal, Gregg, Seastrunk and Cottage Streets remained displaced. Their homes had caught the brunt of the cloud, and would have to have their plumbing, electrical and mechanical systems inspected before they were deemed safe.

An additional 50 residents could not return until the chlorine transfer in the remaining car was complete and the derailment site completely cleared.

They waited, impatient for the word that would send them home.

COMPLETION

THE CHLORINE TRANSFER from the damaged tanker was completed at last. The car was pressure washed inside and out. Later that evening, it was moved onto another rail car for transport from the site.

Graniteville residents watched it go, relieved to finally have it roll away.

The work to repair the tracks would continue for another two days. But the worst — or so residents fervently prayed — was past.

Donnie Williams found his way home. The exterior wiring in his solid Rocktown house had to be replaced, but otherwise, little inside had changed.

Well, Donnie thought philosophically, *the wiring would probably have needed replacing soon, anyway. That's one less thing to worry about.*

Pamela Hall was busy scrubbing down the Hall-Gaffney Learning Center. A professional cleaning crew had been there before her, but Pamela was not satisfied. She wanted to be certain the children returning to her care would be safe, so she cleaned the place from top to bottom, just as she had her home, which had suffered corroded pipes and wiring and a distinct bleaching of its gray siding.

When the children did return to school, Pamela noticed a difference in them. They expressed worries about coming home. Would another accident happen? they wanted to know. Why had this one happened?

Pamela listened to their fears and did her best to address them with calm reassurance. She was relieved most of the children soon regained their composure and behaved as they always had, but she wondered how much of that assurance was real and how much was surface bravado.

She also wondered what the effects of chlorine exposure might be — not just for children, but for all of the Graniteville community — ten years down the road. She could find no one who could give her a definitive answer. No one seemed to know.

Chief Don Turno, Liz Pulver and Ed Schuler returned

to their regular jobs, as did the other members of the Aiken HAZMAT Team. January would turn out to be a big month for them.

Days after dealing with the Graniteville disaster, they were called to help shut down a methamphetamine lab in North Augusta — one of the major busts of the year.

Ed Schuler found the best therapy for dealing with any lingering anxiety from the disaster was in developing a non-profit videotape that would show exactly how horrible a chemical spill could be. Some who viewed it felt the tape was over the top in its graphic photos and audio, but Ed disagreed.

He expressed what he felt in a warning: "The videos, photographs and newspaper clippings you are about to see are intended to show and remind first responders, citizens and political representatives of the devastation hazardous materials can cause a community.

"Those HAZMAT techs, EMTs, firefighters and law enforcement officers that witnessed victims who were overcome by chlorine will always have memories of how terrible a chemical death can be."

AFTERMATH

Pamela Hall and her son, Latrell, stood in the gym of Leavelle McCampbell Middle School, surrounded by neighbors both black and white. Hundreds of survivors of the Graniteville Disaster had gathered in a community-wide service of healing and thanksgiving.

They sang. They worshipped. They hugged each other.

They watched as Our Potter's Hands, the youth group of Graniteville First Baptist Church, presented a dramatic performance.

They gave the GVW volunteers, including Chief Napier, a thunderous standing ovation. The Rev. Barry Antley — whose historic St. James Lutheran Church had been washed in a cloud of vaporized chlorine and survived — served as pastoral representative.

As she stood hand in hand with her son and lifted her voice in the hymn "Holy, Holy, Holy," Pamela was encouraged. Graniteville had come through a dark time, but its people were still strong. They felt each other's pain and comforted each other.

Maybe, in a strange, terrible way, the disaster had been a blessing, Pamela thought.

The people she encountered no longer took life for granted. She knew, from a personal perspective, she would never be so foolish again. Every day was a gift. She understood that now, better than she ever had before.

In every thing, find the blessing, she thought.

It was what she tried to teach the children in her care. It was what she tried to teach Latrell.

She would remember it herself, now.

She hoped all of Graniteville would do the same.

TIMELINE OF EVENTS

COMPILED FROM
AIKEN COUNTY
SHERIFF'S DEPARTMENT
DAILY REPORTS AND
MEDIA SOURCES

DAY 1 — THURSDAY, 1/6/05

• 2:40 a.m.: Head-on collision between Norfolk Southern Train 192 and a parked train.

• Pressurized tanker breaches and 60 tons of chlorine hits the air.

• First 911 call from an Avondale employee.

• First response begins. Volunteer fire fighters, deputies and others attempt to assess the situation and are driven back by chlorine cloud.

• Residents instructed to stay indoors, close doors and windows and turn off ventilation.

• Decontamination sites set up at USC Aiken and Midland Valley High School.

• Avondale Mills suspends operations in Graniteville and nearby Warrenville. Closed: Gregg, Woodhead, Hickman, Swint, Townsend, Graniteville and Warrenville administrative offices, Horse Creek, Warren, Stevens Steam and Sage Mill.

• Eighteen agencies quickly become involved in the initial response, from the Aiken County Sheriff and Aiken Department of Public Safety officers to Emergency Medical Services, DHEC and the FBI.

• 12 noon: Governor Mark Sanford declares state of emergency in Aiken County.

• Curfew imposed from 6 p.m. to 7 p.m. for Graniteville residents within two miles of the wreck.

• Six hospitals between Lexington, S.C., and Augusta, Ga., take in victims.

• Evacuation begins; a dozen residents refuse to leave.

• Norfolk Southern representatives meet with National

Transportation Safety Board officials. Plan to remove 26 undamaged cars from the crash site.

• The U.S. Coast Guard, in cooperation with EPA agrees to send a specialized unit to provide HAZMAT and air monitoring expertise.

• Norfolk Southern establishes assistance center at First Presbyterian Church in Aiken.

• End of Day: Death toll stands at eight.

- Two in Gregg:
  Steven Bagby, 38, of Augusta
  Allen Frazier, 58, of Ridge Spring

- Two in the wooded area around Woodhead:
  Willie C. Shealey, 43, of Graniteville
  John Laird, 24, of North Augusta

- One in the Stevens Steam Plant:
  Rusty Rushton, 41, of Warrenville

- One in truck on Leitner Street:
  Joseph L. Stone, 22, of Quebec, Canada

- One in home on Main Street:
  Tony DeLoach, 56, of Graniteville

- One at crash site:
  Christopher Seeling, 28, West Columbia

DAY 2 — FRIDAY, 1/7/05

• Responders search Woodhead and surrounding area for an unaccounted for employee, but do not find him.

• SRS, DHEC and EPA conduct air quality monitoring. Air around the crash shows low levels of chlorine.

• Telephone calling tree established to account for all Gregg employees; assure no one else is missing.

• Tanker still leaking. Second pressurized tanker is badly damaged. Second release possible.

• Calls begin to hit Animal Services as people worry about their pets.

• Dead fish begin to wash down Little Horse Creek into Langley Pond.

• Curfew nabs four individuals in the evacuation zone.

DAY 3 — SATURDAY 1/8/05

- Search resumes for missing Woodhead employee.
- 2:30 p.m.: Willie L. Tyler, 57, of Aiken, is discovered about 20 yards inside front entrance of Woodhead plant.
- GVW firefighters go back to the Stevens Steam Plant to contain a fire in the coal hopper.
- Trolley Line Road and Laurel Drive reopen. Other barriers squeeze tighter as air quality improves.
- Aiken County Animal Services goes into action to rescue pets in the evacuation zone.
- Aiken County School District decides to close Leavelle-McCampell, Byrd Elementary, Warrenville Elementary, Freedman Parenting Center, the Aiken County Career and Technology Center, and Midland Valley High until Tuesday. Aiken Technical College is also closed because U.S. Highway 1 is shut down.
- 6:40 p.m.: Contractor hired by Norfolk Southern begins to contain and clean up the chlorine spill and wreckage. Crushed lime is scattered to begin neutralizing chlorine on the ground. Empty tankers set into place for transfer of chlorine from remaining tank cars.
- Contractor cobbles steel patch to cover hole in leaking tank. Railroad receives federal approval to move forward with patching ruptured tank car and offloading chlorine and sodium hydroxide from other tankers.
- Evacuation and curfew still in effect.

DAY 4 — SUNDAY 1/9/05

• 12 noon: Contractor places temporary polyethylene patch over tear in the chlorine tank car. Process to off-load lingering chlorine vapors from the tanker begins.

• All Avondale Mills employees finally accounted for.

• Aiken Animal Services has 150 requests for animal retrieval. Aiken Department of Public Safety, Lexington County Animal Control and Clemson University participate in the rescue.

• Aiken/Barnwell Mental Health Center and International Critical Incident Stress Foundation hold series of meetings at USC Aiken to provide information about on-going response and offer crisis counseling. News media asked not to attend so residents can speak freely and without fear.

DAY 5 — MONDAY 1/10/05

• Continuing off-load of 30 tons of chlorine from tanker. Car is turned 90 degrees so solid patch can be installed. • Tanker containing sodium hydroxide moved a short distance from the crash site without incident.

• Workers lay more than 100 feet of temporary track for empty tank cars to off-load 16,000 gallons of chlorine from second tank car.

• Environmental sampling done at Langley Pond and Horse Creek. Chlorine levels in Horse Creek are back to pre-incident levels. Langley Pond levels are slightly higher, but still a low concentration.

• Mail service for evacuated area rerouted to Clearwater Post Office.

• Second meeting at USC Aiken for evacuated residents. Those in need of social services encouraged to call 211.

• Animal rescue continues.

• U.S. DHEC releases guidelines on how to return home safely.

• Evacuation and curfew remain in effect.

• First reports of financial assistance fraud noted by the Aiken County Sheriff's Office.

• Contractor begins transferring chlorine from the second car on the night of Day 5. They cobble on a curved piece of steel to match the contour of tank to produce a permanent patch.

DAY 6 — TUESDAY 1/11/05

- Natural gas leaks detected downtown.
- EPA monitors air quality in Gregg to determine when the building might be reoccupied.
- DHEC and Department of Natural Resources revisit Langley Pond to determine if the kill is large enough to warrant the disposal of dead fish.
- GVW assists in evacuation of a Main Street resident who refused initial evacuation, but now wants to leave.
- Schools plan to reopen Wednesday — all but Leavelle McCampbell, Byrd and Freedman. None are in affected zone, but many students live in the affected area.
- More than 60 people try to get fake licenses. First arrest is made.
- Six pets reported to have died after being returned to their owners.
- The second car is offloaded. Work begins to off-load chlorine from a third car.

DAY 7 — WEDNESDAY 1/12/05

• Twenty-six monitoring units placed to sample the air in affected area. Highest reading is 1.9 parts per million, at the crash site. Monitors remain in place in case of a second disastrous release.

• DHEC and Norfolk Southern develop plan to clean crash site of spilled kaolin and diesel fuel.

• Some Graniteville residents allowed to return home; must show proof of residence at traffic control points. Residents allowed to request home inspections. One-mile evacuation remains in effect for residents closest to hot zone.

• Steel patch is finally completely in place on tanker. Remaining chlorine is off-loaded. Cars can be cleaned before removal from the derailment site.

• Fish kill evaluation is completed. Norfolk Southern arranges for the disposal of dead fish.

• Air monitoring continues. Monitoring conducted at Byrd Elementary and Leavelle-McCampell. Schools are reported clean, as are their buses.

• Partial operations resume at the Swint, Townsend and Horse Creek Divisions of Avondale Mills.

DAY 8 — THURSDAY 1/13/05 & DAY 9 — FRIDAY 1/14/05

- More residents allowed to return home. Home inspections continue.
- Clean up begins on the kaolin spill. Damaged train cars loaded onto flat cars and moved from derailment site. All cars washed prior to departure.
- Track repair is underway.
- Main Street opens between Highway 421 and Aiken-Augusta Highway.
- U.S. EPA Emergency Response Team vet coordinates with Animal Services to organize removal of animal carcasses near crash site.
- Chlorine reading of .7 parts per million at crash site on Friday afternoon; returned to zero within 10 seconds.

DAY 10 — SATURDAY 1/15/05

• Announcement that Byrd and Leavelle McCampbell will open Tuesday. EPA and DHEC conduct air quality and surface testing on both schools. Air is determined safe. All schools scrubbed down from top to bottom.

• More Graniteville residents go home.

• Aiken-Augusta Highway reopened, with one lane only through Graniteville.

• Center for Toxicology and Environmental Health and the U.S. Environmental Protection Agency announce they have conducted nearly 500 home inspections with more planned. All results were negative.

• Thirteen rail cars of scrap metal, paper and other debris prepare leave the area. Norfolk Southern re-rails three locomotives.

• Chlorine transfer continued from damaged rail car.

• Track repair and soil removal continues.

• Aiken Emergency Services reports 550 people sought treatment at area hospitals. 22 remain hospitalized.

• Norfolk reports it will relocate its Local Assistance Center to the former Community Services Building on Ascauga Lake Road the following week. More than 3,000 people have received assistance.

DAY 11 — SUNDAY 1/16/05

• Norfolk moves three locomotives from the site. Two tankers containing sodium hydroxide are on-site for use in the chlorine transfer from the damaged rail car.

• Rail cars carrying freight and debris depart.

• Soil removal at site is complete. Fresh soil is applied at derailment site.

• Park beautification underway; rye and fescue seed applied to the grounds.

• Air and surface sampling completed at Graniteville First Baptist Church, the Aiken County Magistrate Office and the bank complex. No chlorine detected.

• The GVW Fire Department relocates to former Community Services building. Its own headquarters is a mess.

• Fire service and HAZMAT returns to an all-volunteer force.

DAY 12 — MONDAY 1/17/05 — MLK DAY

- Businesses along Main Street given permission to open the following day.
- Seventy-five homes still displaced. Residents must call Aiken County Planning and Development for inspection of plumbing, electrical and mechanical systems. Norfolk Southern will pay for repairs proven to be necessary because of the disaster.
- The USDA will not permit residents of 50 homes to return until chlorine transfer is complete and derailment site deemed safe. This includes Canal Street, Gregg Street, Gentry Street and Cottage Street.

DAY 14 — THURSDAY 1/19/05 & DAY 15 — FRIDAY 1/20/05

• Chlorine transfer from damaged tanker completed. Tanker is pressure washed; moved onto another rail car for transport from the site.

• Norfolk Southern begins operation of community assistance at its new location.

• Track repairs completed in two more days.

INDEX

A

B

C

D

E

F

G

H

I

J

K

L

M

N

O

P

Q

R

S

ABOUT THE AUTHOR

N.J. Nidiffer, a writer and former newspaper reporter, is a personal survivor of the tragedy. She is also responsible for the now-famous photo of the wreck that was seen in numerous national publications, including *The Washington Post*. Nidiffer continues to live in the tight-knit village of Graniteville with her beloved bevy of cats and dogs, also survivors.

OTHER INFORMATIVE TITLES FROM HARBOR HOUSE

100 of the World's Greatest Mysteries
by E. Randall Floyd

Welcome to the Ivory Tower of Babel: Confessions of the Conservative College Professor
by Mike S. Adams

Falling Stars: Air Crashes that Filled Rock & Roll Heaven
by Rich Everitt

The Good, the Bad & the Mad: Weird People in American History
by E. Randall Floyd

In the Realm of Ghosts and Hauntings
by E. Randall Floyd